CW00433497

Chasing Shadows

New York Ghosts

Katya Von Heuser

P.W. Creighton

∞ Introduction ∞

At this time of heightened interest in the paranormal and heightened awareness of the legitimate science behind this research field it becomes increasingly difficult to find a way through the maze of information both for the informed researcher and lay-person alike. There is a significant amount of conflicting information out there and plenty of reading material on the very diverse subjects that fall under the umbrella title of *paranormal.* The first question of any reader, researcher or not, is what makes this book distinct and why should anyone listen to us?

First off who are we and why should you listen to anything we have to say? The New York Shadow Chasers is an organization of professional researchers that utilize the latest scientific methods and technology to document claims of the paranormal. While we are not out to skeptically *debunk* claims, the Shadow

Chasers use legitimate scientific methods that will either validate claims or find the logical explanations for the alleged paranormal activity at a given location simply through practice.

The most distinctive attribute of the Shadow Chasers is the fact that we use the research methods of our dominant academic disciplines, those of in-field anthropology and psychology social sciences researchers. The Shadow Chasers have a host of degrees including Psychology, Anthropology, Environmental Science, Information Technology, Communications and even Education. The team was PBS Television's Ghost Hunters for three years with features on FOX News and in the Haunted NY series of books while hosting seminars on paranormal research for colleges and universities all over the last ten years. The Shadow Chasers are now partnered with Lite 98.7 WLZW in Utica, and conduct a series of tours of historic sites based in Central New York as a means of raising awareness and funding for historic preservation.

The core team of the Shadow Chasers, Phillip and Katharine Creighton, have extensive backgrounds in researching the paranormal and impressive credentials. Phillip Creighton has been researching the paranormal for more than eleven years now, originally beginning this research with a university class at East Tennessee State University that sent him into the field to conduct interviews on Appalachian Folk Medicine that were placed in the Appalachian Archives at ETSU. Once he transferred to SUNY Potsdam, he began to incorporate more geophysics technology into investigations and quickly surpassed the technology described in many ghost hunting guide books at the time. When Phillip relocated to northern New York,, his advisor suggested that he needed more hands on investigations to handle the equipment, so he gathered together a team of like-minded individuals from the university to document claims of the paranormal.

Katharine 'Kate' Creighton had extensive experiences with the paranormal and was attempting to become a ghost hunter on her own utilizing her background in psychology and all the methods that she had read of in the ever growing field of paranormal research. A brilliant and analytical mind, Kate was quick to join the Shadow Chasers and do her best to show everyone that she was a vital asset. After only a few months Kate had learned from a renowned psychic that she was very psychically 'in tune' with spirits and had been for her entire life. Kate attempts to balance her utilization of the technology, psycho-analytic methods and her psychic empathic abilities with the Shadow Chasers to provide the most accurate results on every case.

The Shadow Chasers are professional research organization with a highly skilled team that has been documenting and researching the paranormal for years. The last question is how is this book distinct? This book is culmination of more than eleven years worth of in-field research of paranormal phenomena. After reading new research guides and ghost hunting 'how to' books over the years we have determined that this book will be of the most use and aid for beginning and senior researchers as a guide post with new tips and concepts along with recommendations for creating more professionalism in the field of paranormal research and applying proper science to the field.

Shadow Chasers focuses on Ghostly phenomena and Cryptids (unknown animals) however, there will also be tips for other forms of research. Extensive field tested scientific theories and simple quick answers for Cryptid and Ghostly questions can be found easily here. Readers interested in ghost stories and accounts will find numerous cases, photos and accounts laced throughout as well. This book is intended for all individuals interested in the paranormal in one form or another as a guidepost with quick easy to find information and accounts of in-field research. Enjoy!

∞Discovering the Paranormal∞

Everywhere we look, we are surrounded by people that say that ghosts are scary. Hollywood makes a fortune off of scaring people with ghosts. They are murderous and vengeance ridden, chasing after half-naked teenagers with axes, or dragging sleeping people out of their beds. For what purpose? Generally in the storyline, the motivation isn't important. The main thing is that there is a ghost, and it is terrifying.

To be completely honest, this is a perception that everyone has, Heck, that's something that we even struggle with. It's sometimes scary to be alone in a room, and have the lights suddenly turned off, or to hear someone speak when you're the only one around. Or to walk down a hallway, and have someone grab onto your hand, or poke you in the side, or tug your hair. That is an absolutely terrifying experience.

But why don't we run? It's a question we hear often when we give talks. Someone will raise their hand, and ask what was the scariest thing that happened to us. We'll tell the story of the time we were out in the woods, at a remote cemetery, and a dark shadow began banging at the car as we drove off. Or when we got there, and it hid in the woods, growling at us. Inevitably, someone asks us why we didn't run.

And the answer to that is simple.

Ghosts are like us. With a few rare exceptions, when a location is haunted, it isn't haunted by a monster. It isn't haunted by the angry spirit of a man wielding an axe. It's haunted by someone who once was a mother, or a child, but someone who was loved and cherished, and it's hard to be scared of that. Lots of people will report seeing the spirit of a loved one, and feeling comforted and safe. When you see a spirit, it may not be the spirit of someone you loved, but it is the spirit of someone who was loved.

When someone dies, and becomes a ghost, all they lose is their physical body. If they were kind and caring in real life, it's no different in death. Sure, just like all people aren't good people, there are some spirits who aren't all that nice. But just like among the living those people are rare, they are just as rare among the dead. The problem that occurs is that spirits are limited in how they are able to communicate, so it becomes easy to interpret an expression of interest on their part as an expression of aggression. Sometimes the effect of their actions isn't the intended one. They may mean to touch your arm, but what happens is they grab it hard enough to leave bruises. They aren't intending to hurt you, it just happens accidentally.

So next time you're in a place that's haunted, and the lights turn off, don't think of it as the axe-wielding psycho-spirit making it easier to kill you. Or if you hear someone whispering in your ear, don't assume that what you are hearing are threats instead of words or encouragement. And if you're walking down a hallway, and you feel like something's holding your hand, maybe it's the spirit of a small child, looking for the love they had in life. And if you start to think of it that way, maybe next time you won't be so scared.

Haunted Central New York

History and the paranormal are two subjects that are very closely connected. People who consider the paranormal often feel that if a location has historic significance, it means that it is also haunted. While this is not always true, it is accurate often enough to make historic sites very appealing to those with an interest in the paranormal.

Those interested in the paranormal are very lucky if they happen to live in Central New York. It has a rich history spanning many centuries. Some of the historic events that have taken place in our area are widely known outside of our region. Ask any historian about the Battle of Oriskany or the Erie Canal, and they can recount the many dramatic events associated with these aspects of our nation's history. Part of appreciating the paranormal is learning to look for the subtle history that surrounds us at all times. Take a drive down Genesee Street and look at all the old houses that have been converted into businesses, or look at some of the old abandoned warehouses that are scattered throughout Utica. They may not be nationally known, but they contain a subtle form of history. And who knows? They may also be haunted...

In researching the paranormal or history it is almost a common occurrence to find people who believe a site is haunted whether it is a field, graveyard, home or other structure. A unique aspect of paranormal research is that we may never know all of the 'rules' for paranormal phenomena this is why it is actually possible to have hauntings associated with objects.

Everyone loves antiques but in most cases you don't think of who might still be attached to that object before you bring it home.

There are countless reports of homes and buildings with no reports of hauntings spontaneously having ghostly activity after a 'trigger object' is brought onto the premises. The actual question is whether or not it is triggering a haunting or simply bringing one with it.

On a number of occasions certain objects ranging from Paleolithic arrowheads to 100 year-old Bibles have given off unusual readings during investigations of museums. In a recent investigation of the Collinwood Inn in Oneida the proprietor was a former antiques dealer and actually had activity centered on a number of these antiques. The most curious was an old clock in one of the rooms. As the clock would wind down they would see the apparition of a man near the clock and once the clock actually stopped this apparition would stand in front of the clock and stare at it appearing more and more frequently until the clock was wound again.

Haunted objects or cursed objects, while researching the history of a site can provide insight into why it might be haunted, objects can be much more difficult especially when you have no provenance for the item.

Often when you think of hauntings it conjures images of decrepit old buildings, battlefields and many other sites that can have numerous deaths attributed to the grounds. In general people feel that ghosts are only caused by violent deaths and haunt the place where they died.

In many instances where there are violent deaths there can be hauntings, but it is not the only circumstance. The reason why most people associate ghosts with these locations is because of the grim history that they do possess. It is far more common for people to know of a violent history of a location than a 'quiet' history.

The most common are Revolutionary War and Civil War battlefields. Everyone has heard of the casualties, the deaths that occurred in Gettysburg or even, locally, the Battle of Oriskany. These are historic moments where people died. When someone visits these locations and has an experience with the paranormal, they know it's because of the violent deaths at the location.

When so many people publicly acknowledge the ghostly activity at these sites it fits within the beliefs. Violent death means there will be a haunting. However, this is not always the rule. It's just that we are more likely to hear about the accounts from these locations that have a grim history tied to them. While a house with no reports of violent death can have plenty of activity, people are more inclined to ignore the activity or refuse to acknowledge it because it 'doesn't make sense.'

An old house can just as easily not be haunted as a new house can be haunted. It's not about violent deaths; it's about our ability to tune out the paranormal.

When many hear the words 'ghost' and 'haunting', they think of mist figures of women in white or a shadow figure that darts out of the corner of your vision. While hauntings by former humans are widely reported, and what we are most commonly called in to investigate, they are not the only things that can leave behind an impression. There are numerous cases across the globe of spirit animals; proving that the realm of paranormal research is a formula for surprise.

There are countless reports of owners feeling the presence of their beloved pets after they have passed on. This is most common with, but not exclusive to, companion animals that shared a routine with their owners. Dogs, cats, and horses, in that order, are the most reported animal hauntings. This may simply be because they are the animals people have the most contact with. Many within the public are surprised to learn that animals can even leave a ghost. In the Capitol Theater in Rome, NY a number of people have reported a phantom cat that prowls the premises.

Hauntings can literally come in all shapes and sizes, reminding investigators that the field of paranormal research is an ever changing mystery.

∞Investigating the Paranormal∞

Paranormal Investigations have their roots in the early days of the Spiritualism Movement of the 1800's. During the period fraudulent psychics and spirit photographers were as common as dentists and doctors of the time. The result led to professional detectives, escape artists and researchers to attempt to identify and expose these frauds. Professionals such a Harry Houdini, Sir Arthur Conan Doyle and even Thomas Edison dedicated significant amount of time to discrediting fraudulent psychics and reported paranormal activity.

Today, thanks in-part to Ghost Hunters, paranormal investigations have become a popular hobby for those seeking a bit of adventure. While professional researchers have dedicated a significant amount of their lives earning degrees in related fields and generating academic journals based on their studies. There is a clear distinction between the professional who has dedicated years of their life and the amateur that has an interest in capturing evidence of the paranormal or simply experiencing the phenomena.

There are actually three different approaches to conduct paranormal investigations; analyst, intuitive and documentarian. Each approach carries a different connotation in research circles but each also has a different goal.

The Analyst

The Paranormal Analyst approach to investigations is by-far the most common method taken by would-be ghost hunters. The analyst uses scientific equipment to evaluate the environment and any paranormal phenomena. The analyst approach uses the scientific method and a methodical approach to every investigation. TV shows that employ this method include the likes of Ghost Hunters and Ghost Lab.

The Analyst utilizes equipment like EMF Meters, CCTS Cameras, and Environmental Quality Meters among other technology to document every aspect of the environment so that they can capture any anomalies.

The Analyst Method:

- Conduct Witness Interviews
- Establish Baseline Data (Initial Survey of Site)

- Correlate Witness Accounts with Baseline Data
- Investigation of Site with Survey Equipment
- Correlate Survey Results with Phenomena Captured on Documentary Equipment
- Evaluate Results for False Positives
- Present Findings along with Possible Causes
- Goal - Provide Scientifically Authenticated Objective Evidence

The Intuitive

The Paranormal Intuitive approach to investigations is the oldest methods taken by would-be ghost hunters. The Intuitive relies on subjective impressions of the site, otherwise called the 'psychic intuitive' approach. The intuitive uses their own impressions, experiences and emotional responses to the environment. Sometimes the intuitive may use a basic EMF meter or digital still camera to support their investigation. TV shows that employ this method include the new show The Dead Files.

Intuitive Method:

- Conduct Witness Interviews
- Investigation of Site
- Present Findings
- Goal - Identify the Spirits of the Location and Provide the Reasons Why

The Documentarian

The Documentarian approach to investigations is another longstanding method that has been co-opted for researching the paranormal. The Documentarian relies on professional documentation equipment; cameras, camcorders and audio field recorders in an attempt to document paranormal phenomena. This documentarian uses standard journalism practices and sometimes utilizes specialized equipment or experimental technology to provoke a paranormal response that can be documented. TV shows that employ this method include primarily Ghost Adventures.

Documentarian Method:

- Conduct Witness Interviews
- Review Site History with Witnesses
- Investigation of Site
- Present Findings
- Goal - Capture Paranormal Phenomena on Audio, Video or Digital Stills

Each method can be utilized as the sole means of research. However, many researchers utilize a mixture of these techniques throughout their investigations. This can be complimentary but only so much as the researchers have mastered their default methods and technology.

Why do we investigate?

It's a dark night under a clear sky. The moon is full, and hovers over the old, crumbling building. Even though it's been empty for years, a small white light appears in one window high above. A black shape flits across another, and a scream can be heard dying in the night. This is what paranormal investigators seek, spending countless hours sitting in dark rooms, recording audio, filming and using other technology to measure and detect, waiting patiently for something to happen. But how does someone become interested in investigating? How does someone get the initial urge to look for ghosts? If you pose this question to the paranormal community, odds are there will be many different answers. Some have been searching for years, while others are relatively new to the field. With the birth of paranormal reality TV in the last decade, there has been a surge in popularity and a garnered general interest in the paranormal.

Investigating can be a hobby for some, or even a serious career for others. Some go solo, while others form teams with varying numbers. There are no real accreditations, so this makes it accessible to everyone. However, with no formal professional expectations or limitations set, it can also be easily tarnished or abused.

Because it is a past time that can be enjoyed by the young or old year-round, it is relatable, attainable. Most people have been subjected to a ghost story, myth, or legend, at some point in their lives, whether it's through a friend or family member, or at a campfire tale. Ghosts have purportedly been around for centuries. Even the ancients, Homer, and Virgil, were telling ghost stories, as part of tradition. The stories themselves could be based on a truth, embellished, and long spun out of control, or may be used to incite fear and respect for a location.

People are inherently curious about what happens to us after we die, and this is how ghost stories have become a part of our culture, a part of who we are. This brings about the desire to find answers to the mysteries, and real, tangible evidence to refute the claims or prove them. Some people say they are interested, but never act on it, whereas others will leave their homes, armed with various technical equipment, and spend hours logging data and jotting down personal experiences to analyze later. The people who become investigators have a passion for it, and are drawn to have their own experiences and search for answers. It is an unending quest for the ones who investigate, yet one that is redeeming and fulfilling.

The paranormal community has a kind of black and white dynamic. There are people who adamantly believe in ghosts, and there are people who are more on the skeptic side, who may approach aspects to try and debunk them.

Many want to bring respect to the community, but there's always someone who will resort to devious claims in order to gain attention. From faking evidence, to committing various types of fraud, these are the ones who can pull the paranormal community down into the depths of doubt and non-credibility. To the skeptics, our work is foolish and unnecessary, and we work hard to establish a sense of professionalism and respect for us, for the field, and for others like us. It only takes one bad example to tarnish many reputations and it's incredibly hard to regain the respect.

That being said, I feel that most of us are out there, spending our nights diligently looking for answers, sacrificing our time and sleep because we truly love it. The few, who are nefarious, while they can't be avoided, can be counteracted. Perseverance will show that our work is legitimate and worthy of respect.

Becoming an Investigator:

The number one question we are always asked when we are giving a presentation or interview is always; "How do you become a ghost hunter?"

In truth, for each of our team we have our own personal reasons that drive us to do the work but the deeper question is how one learns to be a paranormal investigator. The first words that roll out of anyone's mouth are "There is no such thing as a certified paranormal investigator." Then you take one look around the web for teams in your region.

You find dozens of ghost hunters claiming to offer "certification" through a paid training course with the team in the field or even find "T.A.P.S. Certified Family" logos tagged to their pages.

If there is no such thing as a certified investigator then why are so many teams clamoring for approval? Why are they selling certification? What does it take to become a legitimate paranormal investigator?

Fallacy #1

The very first fallacy to address is that there are no professional or certified investigators. Anyone attempting to argue this as fact has not done their homework. Even worse, they have forgotten the legitimate researchers who have been in the field for decades.

Professionals Investigating the Paranormal:

Parapsychologists - These individuals are licensed psychologists with PhDs. Most are Professors working for or researching for highly respected Universities including the likes of Princeton, Duke and even Edinburgh.

Anthropologists - These individuals are professionals tasked with recording oral traditions and studying the dynamics of cultures. In order to practice in the public sphere and work with human subjects these individuals are required to obtain university ethics certifications.

Psychologists/Sociologists - These individuals are professionals tasked with studying individual or social behavior. In order to practice in the public sphere and work with human subjects these individuals are required to obtain university ethics certifications. Most psychologists are required to be licensed.

Environmental Survey Technicians - These individuals are scientists with specializations ranging from geophysics to meteorology. All are scientists that are trained in environmental analysis.

While Parapsychologists are the only true professional 'paranormal investigator,' the methods used by these other professionals more than qualify them for any paranormal investigation. If you remove the paranormal from the equation all of these professionals would be licensed or certified experts that could be called upon.

However, when you add the paranormal to the equation you can no longer have an expert. But you do have a professional expert in a given methodology. Try telling a licensed parapsychologist or Environmental Geologist that they are not experts at what they are doing.

Fallacy #2

The second most common fallacy is that it takes years of training to be a paranormal investigator. While any of the professionals that I mentioned previously have spent years if not a good portion of their lives dedicated to the studies of a particular field to be an amateur paranormal investigator it only takes a modicum of training, a lot of resources and dedication to become a ghost hunter.

There are only a few things you need:

Know the Scientific Method

- Define the question
- Gather information and resources (observe)
- Form hypothesis
- Perform experiment and collect data
- Analyze data
- Interpret data and draw conclusions that serve as a starting point for new hypothesis
- Publish results

- Retest (frequently done by other scientists)

Know Occam's Razor. This is a principle that generally recommends selecting the competing hypothesis that makes the fewest new assumptions, when the hypotheses are equal in other respects.

Be objective. An investigator and a scientist are objective. If you set out with the mind to prove or disprove/"Debunk" then you inherently introduce bias into the research.

Absorb as much on the subject as possible. Read. TV does not teach you principles or methods. The more you read the more resources you have and you'll have a better perspective to judge both your own and other's work.

Work with others in your chosen area, meet with and work with as many teams in the area as you can. See how each team works, learn their methods, and learn their perspectives.

∞Ethics of Paranormal Investigating∞

There are many recently founded paranormal research organizations. A long term interest in the paranormal, supernatural or occult mixed with the popularity of paranormal shows today has given rise to a great many amateur investigative teams. While the majority of new investigators rely on TV for their standards of behavior and methods it is important to note that TV tends to edit out the 'boring' parts. Just as well we have encountered many teams that have questionable ethics a lack of real protocol and dubious procedures. Not all investigators chose this route but the lack of any formal training or any official guidelines leave the investigators with nothing to judge their 'standards' by except what they see or can cut and paste on the web.

Ethics should be the first staple of any investigation team. These are not only the guidelines for behavior at an investigation but also statements of expectations for the investigators. We have seen amateur investigators go public with private case evidence before even reporting it to the client, we have encountered teams that trespass on private property without hesitation, we have had teams 'help' one client only to shift the problems to another and refuse to accept responsibility, we have heard teams slander another team to clients.

Ethics should not include some random assortment of 'investigators should not take photos while driving....' This is not an ethic; this is an expectation from founders. All researchers should be expected to sign a waiver agreeing to this code of ethics and the founder(s) are responsible for assuring others are held to it.

Protocol is another area in which we have seen many failures with investigators. Similar to ethics, protocol is a professional guide stating an investigator's foundation for their research. Again, this is not some quick 'how we work' cut and paste guide. Professional research protocols state your purpose for the research, the origins of the research, your methods used in the research and detailed explanations of what the investigator(s) goal is.

Procedure is another area we find that a great many teams are lacking. We have seen many investigators that just don't know what to do. They want to be 'Ghost Hunters' so badly they don't care what it takes to get there. We have seen investigators time and again have miss-aligned priorities. These investigators commonly put their own goals ahead of even the most common standards of research. The first thing the team ever invests in is something to promote group cohesion, such as spending all of their funding on t-shirts, car magnets, banners, signs and all manner of promotional items to 'get their name out there.' When forming an investigative team, the first purchases should be for investigative equipment, whether this is EMF meters, cameras, or audio recorders.

This is not an issue with a team that is well-established, but if the team is recently founded and only has a couple of cameras and one surveying instrument between them it becomes a severe issue of credibility. All of the funding that was funneled into promotions could have been used to purchase more equipment to increase options in their methods. Teams that are well-established have gotten their name out there for their work, not because of their marketing ability.

The question is, would you prefer a group of amateurs to investigate YOUR home with nothing but cameras and uniform t-shirts or would you prefer a team with extensive research capabilities, equipment and knowledge? An amateur team can fall into either category.

In reality, any amateur ghost hunting team can hold to professional Ethics, Protocols and Procedures. The problem is most investigators do not have anything to compare their standards to except for what is out on the web. If an investigator is just starting out it is our belief that they should aim for the highest standards. If they are out for a thrill or a club it shows in their standards. What separate a professional from an amateur is the ethics and standards they adhere to.

Shadow Chasers Case Files:

On May 21st the Shadow Chasers teamed up with several affiliate members to investigate the Rolling Hills Asylum in East Bethany, New York.

      While we have been in service since 2002, we have never been ones to target prestige locations, and in-fact we have had nearly 90% of all of our cases come to us. This was to be our second 'Paranormal Road Trip.' The site was notoriously haunted and well within driving distance. The team unanimously decided it would be worth our time and an investment to investigate one of America's most notoriously haunted locations.

History:

Originally, a carriage house and tavern servicing stage coaches stood there from 1790 until December 1826, when it was sold to Genesse County. The carriage house still stands on the property today. The tavern serviced travelers from Batavia, NY to Warsaw, NY traveling along what is now known as US Route 20. At that point, the facility took in paupers, unwed mothers, the insane, and orphans.

By the early 1950s, the facility served only as a nursing home, where it was then closed by 1972; stepping aside for a new facility in Batavia, NY.

After which, the building stood empty until 1992, when it was re-opened as Carriage Village, a mall of unique shops. Since then it has transformed into a paranormal investigation hot spot and has been operating public and private ghost hunting tours, paranormal investigations, historical tours and even special events.

Planning Phase:

In most investigations you contact the proprietor and work with them to set up an ideal investigation date. One look at the Rolling Hills Asylum website and we were a little dubious about the credibility of the site. We proceeded to plan the investigation assuming that site was attempting to blend with clichés that are so prevalent in the paranormal community. We contacted the proprietor regarding a date and were quickly lost in confusion. The proprietor had established different names for the investigation types and had confused the names as well. This did not bode well. After some delayed conversations and re-directs to their website calendar we established a date and locked in our investigation.

From the RHA website:

Plan to arrive 15 minutes early.

This affords you enough time to park your vehicles, gather all your equipment, and be in line with your Valid ID and Payment Confirmation

 The faster we are able to check you in, the quicker you will begin the tour, and the sooner you will be able to investigate. There will always be at least two RHA™ representatives in the buildings at all times.

Time and date were established for the 21st at 9PM-5AM. A few days before hand the proprietor contacted us via email saying that there were still openings and if we wanted she could set it up. We had to inform her that we had already established a date and paid. She responded by saying that she still had openings on that date if we were still interested. We responded again and finally believed we had everything straightened out.

She informed us that we need to make sure we were there 15min before 9PM with our receipt.

Road Trip:

We set out from Utica at 3PM and met up with our first affiliate member, Vivian, in Syracuse. Continuing on from there we discussed the history of the location and all of the reported activity from the site. Investigations by Ghost Adventures, Ghost Hunters and all of the shows that discussed Rolling Hills Asylum from the History Channel to the Travel Channel all claimed extensive history and activity on the site. We arrived in Batavia, NY at just before 6PM. Since we were less than 30min from Rolling Hills it seemed like a good time to stop for dinner.

After dinner we stopped to pick up some sodas and snacks for the investigation. We double checked the website making sure we were on schedule. According to the site we still had an hour and a half before we had to be at the site but we assumed it would be okay to arrive early. Then we received a call from our other affiliate who was already on-site. The proprietor said that if we were not there in 15 minutes we would not be allowed in the building.

On Site:

Fortunately we arrived with time to spare. On-site the proprietor snapped at us for 'not filling out the online form for each for each of us.' (There was only one form if you were purchasing for a team).

We showed the proprietor our information along with the current website information. Her response was "She doesn't need to be told what's on the site. She's the one that put it there and we were wrong.' This really didn't bode well at all. The proprietor also informed everyone that no outside food or drink would be allowed on the premises.

We were admitted into the building and had to fill out the requisite waivers for the investigation. Our base would be the 'Green Room' where everyone's equipment would be left and where we could grab coffee. The proprietor then took everyone on a tour of the building describing the history and the activity at the various locations throughout the structure.

This was not allowed to be filmed or photographed, and the proprietor recounted a number of inaccurate facts about the site, and led everyone through a series of 'staged' rooms. Most consisted of furniture found at the local dump and were accessorized with countless Halloween decorations such as fake cockroaches, bats and rats. The tour lasted more than 2 hours after which the proprietor essentially turned everyone loose to investigate. No coordination, no oversight, just 'go do something.' The only restrictions were no bright flashlights, no 2-way radios, and no trips to the bathroom (port-a-potty) without escort.

Investigation:

We opened our investigation by dividing into two teams. Kate, Courtinie and Vivian started in the basement area while Josh, Sean and Phil started on the first floor.

The investigation was fairly straight forward except for audio. Every time we would attempt an EVP or even investigate the odd room we would receive audio contamination from one of the Rolling Hills staff elsewhere in the building. Worst still was rounding a corner and almost running into one of Rolling Hills staff that was standing in the shadows just chatting with each other.

After an hour the two teams met up and actually focused on the 'Boiler Room'. Together we started to document interactions and even captured a moving mist on the Full Spectrum camera, but once again our EVP session was sabotaged by the volunteer staff chatting elsewhere in the building.

Due to the size of the structure the team was able to keep somewhat localized after the basement and all work on a single floor together. We investigated throughout the basement, morgue and laundry room. In the laundry room we managed to capture some activity, some interactions with the equipment, and even captured several EVPs.

After a couple of hours our team needed to regroup and grab some additional batteries as well as some additional equipment before proceeding but when we returned to the 'Green Room' we found the doors locked and no one around. We were forced to make due for almost 2 hours before we could get to our equipment.

Continuing our investigation in the East Wing, we were able to document countless audible phenomena that sounded like footsteps and dragging desks that were coming from rooms while we were in them. One of the most curious reported phenomena was from the lounge at the end of the floor where the proprietor had explained that a spirit would stand in-front of one of the door windows while the doors were closed. An unknown psychic had informed her that the spirit was 'Jack' and he was aggressive.

Initial impressions were that it was an optical illusion caused by stereoscopic vision. Utilizing a Laser Net from the lounge against the windows with Josh and Phil in the lounge we were able to rule out paranormal phenomena as the cause for the shadow window. The audible phenomena from the surrounding rooms, including footsteps in the hallway were quite amazing. As we re-grouped we headed back for our equipment and found it locked yet again.

We headed to the third floor where we began our investigation of the 'Ruthless Nurse' but found yet more volunteer staff, and they actually slammed the door closed on us to prevent us from investigating the nurse's room.

Despite the countless reports of activity from the location, we really did not find any anomalous readings or activity from the third floor. The PX did respond to questions in one of the rooms but there was no real activity. We retreated back to the 'Green Room' and retrieved some much needed coffee and equipment while we discussed the next phase.

After deliberation we returned to the second floor wing where we had documented the noises, but this time we did not capture any more additional EVPs.

We decided to focus on the Boiler Room where we had also captured activity previously. As we entered the room we caught the roiling black mist on the Full Spectrum camera again.

Once more our EVP session was interrupted by the volunteer staff talking elsewhere but we did start to receive responses on our PX that coincided with static spikes on the SAII.

The Wrap Up:

Our investigation of Rolling Hills Asylum concluded without further incident. We packed our equipment, headed out to the cars and were promptly locked from the building. The Shadow Chasers investigation of Rolling Hills Asylum was certainly an adventure.

We captured a number of audible phenomena on both audio recorders and video. We captured a few interesting photographs and had a number of experiences. Would we want to go back and investigate Rolling Hills Asylum again? The definitive answer is No.

Between the staged rooms, the fraudulent facts and the general attitude of the proprietor, Rolling Hills does indeed have some ghostly activity but nowhere near the legendary accounts.

Even Ghost Hunters and Ghost Adventures captured limited evidence from the location. The proprietor has embellished many accounts, deceived investigators and currently claims that she has a 'team' that investigates the site regularly. When asked how they investigate, the proprietor responded by saying they use a 'Franks Box (Spirit Box) and a K2 meter. These are two of the most questionable devices at an investigator's disposal today.

The largest offense though has to do with the attitude towards her clients and the horrifically inaccurate history that she recounts to investigators. Question the Genessee County Historical Society if you want to know the true history of the location.

Rolling Hills Asylum is known for its haunted activity, its legends, and has become a Mecca for paranormal investigators, but it is more subject to marketing and monetary motives than most locations.

Experiencing a prestige location is definitely a unique experience but Rolling Hills was not worth the hassle or price of admission. From Salem, Massachusetts to Gettysburg, Pennsylvania there are countless historic sites that have turned to the paranormal and respect their clients. Rolling Hills is not one of them. The proprietor and subsequently the site are what our friend at Haunt Jaunts has dubbed a "Paranormal Poser."

∞Capturing the Paranormal∞

When it comes to field research, photography is un-avoidable, however most simply do not understand the basic principles of photography let alone what camera they need for the job. How is it possible to select the best camera if one doesn't understand the requirements needed of the camera?

Since the Spiritualism Movement in the 19th century, the phenomena of Spirit Photography, essentially capturing ghosts on film, has been a staple of paranormal research. In truth, photography is not merely limited to spirit photography though, it is a staple of all research fields from Geology to Anthropology and everything in-between.

In all instances of using photography as research it is of the utmost importance to understand the basic principles of photography. This means knowing what your optics, aperture, shutter and sensor can do for your shots. Every camera is different and knowing the affects of what changing one aspect to the equation can do is fundamental.

Paranormal Photography isn't just for the amateur ghost hunter but also for those needing to take clear pictures of cryptids (mysterious animals like Bigfoot) and even UFO hunters. All aspects of these research fields make any evidence suspect, so it is extremely important to produce photographs that are almost beyond reproach.

Most paranormal photographs are taken either in haste or most frequently, under low lighting conditions. As such, the most useful skill for any researcher to have is the ability to take excellent photos under those conditions.

Low Light Photography:

When taking photos under low lighting conditions, be it ghosts and spirit photography or UFOs or the mysterious animal rampaging through your backyard there are five basic tips you need to keep in mind to take the best possible shots.

1.   **Use a Flash** - While the flash will front-light a subject it can also wash-out your subject. The built-in flash on most cameras is also restricted in distance. Most can only reach about 15ft distance effectively under the best conditions. This is why it is good to use supporting lights or an external flash. If you are taking a photo through a window or other reflective surface it is best to shut off the flash or remove the reflective surface to eliminate lens flare.

2.   **Steady the Camera** - Under low lighting conditions the camera is required to keep the shutter open longer to obtain an image. Even if there is the slightest movement it can create blur or more commonly, light-paintings. To take shots under these conditions either equip a tripod/monopod and most importantly, stop moving.

3.   **Open Your Aperture** - The wider the aperture the more light the camera can take in and thus, the clearer the image. This is also why point 2. is so important. Most point-and-shoot cameras set on auto will do this but will not warn about motion blur and light painting.

4.   **Boost Your ISO** - Most know their ISO as 'Film Speed.' Increasing your ISO will reduce the amount of time needed to keep the shutter open and reduce the chances of causing motion blur. Typically, you will need 400 or 800 ISO however it may be necessary to raise your ISO to 1600 or more but the higher you raise the ISO above 800 the more you increase the 'noise' in your shots.

5.   **Shoot in Burst Mode** - Burst mode will allow you to take a series of shots, 3, 5 or continuous so long as the shutter button is held. The downside of this mode is that the built-in flash will be disabled because it cannot fire as rapidly.

The Best Camera for Paranormal Photography

While almost any modern camera can be utilized for paranormal photography under low-lighting or rapid fire conditions, there are quite a few cameras that a number of ghost hunting and UFO outfitters have been selling that are far from effective.

SVP/Vivitar - These cameras are extremely low quality and are incapable of taking any photos under low-lighting conditions or even fast movement. These cameras are so low quality that even under perfect bight lighting conditions they will create artifacting and ghosting (motion blur) of subjects.

Due to their cheap nature and low quality many enterprising individuals have taken to modifying these cameras for low light and 'full spectrum.' Sadly, even this cannot save these cameras and the quality of the sensor is still the same regardless of what light spectrum they can see into.

Fujifilm - While some people adamantly defend this brand and they do make some decent cameras for everyday use, the brand on a whole typically fails to create solid low-light performance. Most cameras are subject to poor low-light performance, creating artifacting and ghosting. More recently the Fujifilm X10 was recalled because the sensor was creating white orbs on every shot taken.

Curiously, another camera with poor low-light performance was taken and modified by the ghost hunting outfitter community and is now sold as a Full Spectrum or 'Para-Spectrum' camera. Even if you do capture a full-body apparition on this camera who would ever believe it with such a suspect camera in your hands?

Choosing the Perfect Camera

So what is the perfect camera for ghost hunting? What is the perfect camera for UFOs? What camera should you use to capture Bigfoot or Champ or Nessie or even that suspect Chupacabras?

Well, there is no real wrong answer. If you're looking for the perfect low-lighting camera that's a point-and-shoot then you have a multitude of options but you can narrow it down based on the conditions you need to operate in out in the field.

Low Light - Typically you want something that can take quality shots at night or under low lighting conditions.

Fast - You want something that can boot up quickly and take clear shots just as quickly.

Easy to Use - You do not want to fuss with settings when your subject can be gone in milliseconds. Lenses and Auto-Focus can be the bane of your existence in the wrong conditions.

Durable - Yes that DSLR may be a thing of beauty and you may be dynamite with it but it is far too easy to have a camera knocked from your grip, banged into something or even clogged with dust. Do you really want to risk that camera and those lenses you saved up for on someone's dingy basement? All it takes is a stray nail to ruin a $300 lens and your day.

After looking at these requirements there are a number of cameras out there that still fit the bill and most prominently Sony and Canon seem to rule the low-light and durability categories. Digital point-and-shoots like the Sony Cybershot TX10 and the Canon Powershot D10 can work wonders and also be used on your vacation too.

Time and again we hear of things called 'Orbs' being given as photographic evidence of paranormal activity or being dismissed as anything other than dust. While there are many possibilities in photography and videography I think it's necessary re-analyze these phenomena.

Visually, 'Orb' phenomena have a variety of possibilities that are far from paranormal. Orbs are described as perfectly circular artifacts that appear in photos or on video. These can be a variety of colors, angular or even distorted in some fashion. All of these 'orbs' are simple artifacts in some sense and on video these tend to drift or move through the area. These can be photographic errors, weather, dust, or can actually be paranormal in origin.

Photographic errors:

Relying on digital cameras has created a rise in 'Orbs phenomena.' All digital cameras and camcorders have a processor called a 'Charged Couple Device' or CCD chip; this processor takes what the lens sees and turns it into an electrical impression that can be displayed as the image/video. Under low-lighting conditions without specific modifications (IR, UV, Flash etc) the CCD will fail to process portions of the image creating blank spots in the image/video. These look just like it sounds completely blank portions of the image usually in large circles.

Environmental:

Weather like rain, snow or even fog can create 'Orbs' on your images and video. These may have a look of intelligence or direction thanks in part to things like wind or even breathing. These can be easily recognized by the distorted nature of the particulate. Under close examination none of these will appear as perfect circles or have the specific attributes of paranormal.

Dust will have the same attributes as weather including distortion. The unique attributes to dust are that it tends to appear in clusters, each 'orb' is semi-transparent and usually brown or grey in color.

Paranormal:

These 'orb phenomena' appear as perfectly circular blobs of light usually blue/white or red/white in color. These can also range from nearly transparent to entirely opaque. The closer these are to transparent the more detail you will be able to see in the nucleus that usually consists of a kaleidoscope pattern. The most defining feature is there is perfect 'halo' around the individual orb of one solid color. For example, a white orb will have a perfectly blue ring around it.

Now these can show distortion as well due to motion (low shutter speed) but close examination will show all of the traits described.

Concepts:

A paranormal 'Orb' has been hypothesized to be a ghost. It is believed that since a sphere is the most efficient form of energy usage ghosts compress their energy into this shape to move/linger. Another hypothesis has 'orbs' as a sign of ghostly or paranormal activity.

Through testing we have established that these paranormal 'orb phenomena' are actually static electricity/Ionized Air that is found near paranormal phenomena. These are essentially 'spin-off' from ghostly entities. The color/opaqueness of the orb is determined by the voltage of the orb. Higher voltage results in more defined 'orbs'.

Further testing along these lines has also demonstrated to us that when an orb is captured in motion if you turn back to the source/direction it came from you will actually capture the apparition/source.

Haunted Central New York

One local haunted site is Erie Canal Village. For readers not familiar with this popular school field trip site, it is the recreation of a typical village found along the banks of the Erie Canal, and reflecting homes commonly built before the creation of the canal, during the digging, and when the canal was a prosperous method of conducting trade. Erie Canal Village's buildings are not original to the site (which was also the location of Fort Bull, active during the French and Indian War), but are instead moved there from various small towns scattered throughout the Mohawk Valley.

There are many reported hauntings on the site of Erie Canal Village. Some reports stem from the site of Ft. Bull, the location of a horrific massacre by French-Canadians. There are reports of footsteps and full bodied apparitions in the barn turned into a carriage museum. There have been reports of strange noises in the train depot, as well as in the tavern.

When there are hauntings reported in a location like this, there is one question that is asked: what is haunted? Is it the land that is haunted? Undoubtedly, the events that took place at Fort Bull are more than enough to cause spirits to linger. But the spirits inside of the buildings themselves seem to orient themselves to the buildings. So, are the buildings haunted by spirits that have followed them to their new home? Were the buildings haunted prior to being moved to this land? Is it the combination of a specific location and a specific building that cause the hauntings to occur?

Shadow Chasers Case Files:

In the early 1800s, travel was difficult in New York State. There was a lack of natural rivers that lent themselves to water travel, and the condition of the roads at that time was poor. Travel was a long, grueling process, and commerce in New York State suffered for it.

In 1817, ground was broken on an innovative new way of travel in New York State. The Erie Canal was being constructed, a giant man-made river spanning from Albany to Buffalo, revitalizing commerce in the state, and making transportation easier.

Erie Canal Village was built on the site of the initial stretch of the Erie Canal, and is a living history museum designed to demonstrate what life was like prior to the Erie Canal, and demonstrating the prosperity that increased trade brought to the central New York area.

Erie Canal Village is made up of buildings obtained from throughout central New York. There is a small one-room schoolhouse to demonstrate what the educational system was like in the 1800s, a church, and a general store. There is also a tavern located on the property, which serves as a good example of the local meeting spot and resting place for weary travelers from the Canal. Erie Canal Village not only focuses on the lifestyle of residents in canal-side homes, but they also have a museum dedicated to various forms of wagons, an old cheese factory, as well as a railroad station.

The homes located at Erie Canal Village showcase various eras during the time of the Erie Canal. One home dates to just before the creation of the Erie Canal. It is a small home, with few luxuries, demonstrating the simplicity created by the difficulty of travel and trading. The second home dates to the beginning of the Erie Canal, when trading was starting to become easier. The home is larger and better furnished. The final home on the site is a large Victorian Home. While currently being renovated, this home demonstrates the luxuries that the Erie Canal brought to the central New York region.

Not to be forgotten is the site of Fort Bull. In use during the French and Indian War, it was the site of a horrible massacre imparted by French soldiers moving south from Canada. A monument stands in the location of Fort Bull in memory of the lost soldiers.

The Shadow Chasers began their investigation with the tavern. After completing a walkthrough we were drawn back to the building after seeing a shadow moving in one of the windows. We would obtain EVPs and odd EMF readings during our investigation of the building. After the tavern, we moved on to the train station, with no results, and then to the barn holding the wagon collection, the Carriage Museum. There we obtained several EVPs, and observed oddly moving shadows.

Continuing forward to the school house we witnessed a strange blue light near the Victorian home, but disappeared when approached and could not identify a source of the anomaly. Resuming our investigation of the school house, we were able to audibly hear phantom knocks and captured additional EVPs in the building. Finishing with the school house the team progressed to the church.

No results were obtained in the church, but high EMF was measured when we investigated the site of Fort Bull. We investigated the remaining buildings with minimal activity observed, until we reached the general store, the last stop of the evening. There we measured high EMF and strange equipment activity, as well as EVPs, and flashlight and PX responses in answer to questions asked by investigators.

∞Videotaping the Paranormal∞

Many people are drawn into ghost hunting and paranormal research by the numerous shows that flood the air these days but even more people fail at the basics of documentation especially when it comes to footage.

Countless amateur investigators are interested because it gives them a chance to be on adventure, others want to understand and still more want to be their own star. Sure it is all well-and-good to help a home owner understand what's going on in their home but for the few investigators that are documentarians at heart, an investigation is a chance to preserve history. Many stories, accounts and legends have never been recorded and just as frequently historic sites have never had their history documented on video.

Paranormal Investigating, ghost hunting, especially at historic sites is the perfect chance for a budding videographer to preserve history and get in some quality video work under rather 'unusual' circumstances.

What is a Paranormal Videographer?

A Paranormal Videographer is your team's dedicated camera man (or woman). Everyone that carries a camcorder should have a working knowledge of the camera and basic videography techniques. It is paramount for everyone who picks up a camera to know basic videography.

Videography Basics

Know Your Camera - This is the fundamental for everyone who picks up a camera. The more sophisticated the camera, the more you'll need to know about its proper operation.

When filming keep the 5 Deadly sins of film-making in check:

- **Do not 'Firehose' your shots.** Use your eyes to see where you want to pan the camera to and then smoothly pan the camera in that direction.
- **Avoid 'Jog' in your shots as much as possible.** Try to keep the camera as smooth and level as possible even when moving to prevent 'Blair Witch' videos. Use shoulder mounts, support grips and harnesses to keep footage clean and professional.
- **Watch your lighting, avoid back-lighting subjects.** Adjust your perspective so that your subject is well lit.
- **When filming people avoid giving no lead or nose room in your shots.**

Make sure your subject is properly framed within the shot.

- **Frame subjects appropriately, avoid cutting off chins.**

Know what lighting you need and how it affects your shots. Too much light and you'll have artifacting on your lens. Too little and your processor will cause moiré and artifacting.

Sound can be the hardest thing to control when shooting but it can also be the strongest piece of your shot.

Lighting

When shooting in low lighting conditions it is necessary to manipulate environmental lighting or create artificial light. Most cameras can only process a given scene with a specific minimum requirement. Other cameras that are modified for infrared or night vision still require a lighting source to meet the minimum requirements for imaging.

Artificial sources include: lamps, typically on-board lights that are built into the camera; spot lamps, lights that are usually attached that project a focused beam in a direction; and finally floodlights, accessory lights that give diffuse lighting to a general direction.

There are two types of light source today; the halogen that produces warm light; and LED that produces a cold white light.

For Night Vision camcorders these elements still hold true however the light that is produced is created with infrared light.

Audio

One of the strongest elements and most difficult to perfect is audio. As any videographer can tell you, developing audio and perfecting audio are almost impossible while in the field. The best practice, as with any part of videography is to practice redundancy.

In the field audio can be obtained through one of three means, onboard, inline and external sources.

All cameras have built-in or onboard microphones to record audio the problem is that most of these, regardless of the quality of camera, are still insufficient for most purposes. Onboard microphones tend to pick up the internal workings of the camera.

Higher-quality cameras allow for the use of inline microphones. These include shotgun microphones and wireless microphone packs. These often rely on XLR inputs and phantom power so that there is little loss in quality of the audio.

External audio relies on audio recording sources that are separate from the camera and is only functional for post-production purposes.

The best way to obtain usable audio in the field is to monitor your levels. This means on cameras that support it, you can listen to the audio as it is being recorded and watch the channels on the camera for clipping. Even the Mitsuba HDC 505 allows you to listen to your audio as you're recording.

As a paranormal videographer, monitoring audio can be the most productive time while in the field because not only can your camera indicate if you received an EVP but also depending on the model it could also indicate the direction that the EVP came from in the field.

Videography in the Field

When you're in the field on a paranormal investigation it is important to note that the videographer is not present to capture evidence but record the witness accounts and document the investigation of the site.

To produce the best possible video for an investigation it is necessary to keep the camera stable through the use of tripod or support brackets like shoulder mounts. Not only do these help keep the picture steady but also alleviate the fatigue that comes with carrying the camera for hours.

In video post-production remember that the more you edit the footage, the more you adjust it to make it 'look better,' the more questionable the footage will be to the rest of the world. This is why it is better to produce the best footage in-the field and skip the post edits.

When it comes to ghost hunting, the most fundamental piece of technology is that of IR camcorders. Regardless of whether a team utilizes CTS cameras or just relies on a multitude of camcorders on tripods, if you're shooting under low lighting conditions you need an infrared camcorder.

Over the years we've encountered a number of very ambitious people that have created their own gear out of components, and modifying readily available equipment. Now, some of these people are pretty outstanding and create some very intriguing pieces of ghost hunting equipment like the 'Tri-Field Audio-Visual Recorder" but the fact of the matter is that if you want to shoot at night you will need an actual camcorder.

The advantage of selecting a genuine camcorder with nightshot or IR capabilities means it does not have to be restricted to just ghost hunting work or night time shooting. You can actually take the camera to your daughter's play and have a good video to show for it, providing you choose wisely.

Interestingly enough, it may seem like IR camcorders are hard to find but this is not the case. There are a multitude of options available but between the various confusing model numbers and rather random camcorders that appear after an Amazon or Google shopping search for 'IR Camera' it may seem like there are only a few. So rather than roughly telling a brand and saying what you might find, we've assembled a complete list of the top camcorders ranging from the amateur price level to the professional camcorders used on Ghost Adventures, Ghost Hunters, Destination Truth and Haunted Collector.

Budget Camcorders with IR

These cameras are commonly sold by ghost hunting outfitters and are often cheap, flimsy and are poor quality recording. Prices range from $39.99 - 159.99

Vivitar DVR 510n - 5.1 MP - supported memory: SD, SDHC - flash card

Vivitar DVR 560 - 5.1 MP - supported memory: SD, SDHC - flash card

Bell & Howell DNV 900HD - 1080p Full HD Camcorder that can capture 20 hours of video (based on card).

Older Budget Camcorders with IR

These camcorders are becoming harder to find but are some of the best camcorders to use for any low-light work and can still be found on Amazon or eBay. These are former high-end consumer camcorders. Prices range from $100.00 - 500.00

Sony DCR SR 40 - 30GB hard disk drive, high-quality stills and videos.

Sony DCR SR 42 - 30GB hard disk drive, high-quality stills and videos.

Sony DCR SR 60 - 30GB hard disk drive, high-quality stills and videos.

Sony DCR SR 82 - 60 GB hard disk drive, 40 hours of video and stills.

Best Consumer IR Camcorders

These night vision camcorders are the best available consumer camcorders with infrared capabilities, often nightshot or 'twilight' shooting modes. Prices range from $299.00 - 799.00

Sony HDR - CX 190 - 1920x1080 Full HD video and 5.3 MP pictures with back-illuminated Exmor CMOS sensor. This is one of the confirmed camcorders used by Ghost Adventures as a 'Static X Camera.'

Sony HDR - XR 260V - 1920 x 1080 Full HD and 8.9 MP pictures, 60p recording and playback - This is the new model used by Ghost Adventures for the 2012 season.

Canon VIXIA HFR 300 - 1920 x 1080 Full HD, 24p and 30p record modes, flash memory

Canon VIXIA HFR 32 - 1920 x 1080 Full HD, 24p and 30p record modes, flash memory

Panasonic HDC TM80 - 1920 x 1080 Full HD, OIS, and IRT Tech

Canon - LEGRIA HF G10 - 1920 x 1080 Full HD, HD and Flash Memory, High optical resolution, 1.5lux

Best Prosumer & Professional IR Camcorders

These night vision camcorders are very high-end producing the best results and are frequently used in video production by the larger televised ghost hunters including Ghost Hunters, Ghost Hunters international, Haunted Collector and Ghost Adventures. While these cameras are outstanding they also reflect the prosumer price level and are not typically within a normal person's budget. These range in price from $2500 and up.

Canon XF 100 - Professional Camcorder with all professional features, records to flash memory

Canon XA10 - The XA10 Professional Camcorder allows users to record up to 24 hours of clear high definition video to a 64GB internal flash drive or to two SDXC-compatible memory slots. With Relay Recording, the camcorder automatically switches video recording from the internal drive to the SD memory cards when the memory becomes full. This Camcorder is currently used on "Haunted Collector" to film the night vision segments.

Panasonic AG DVC 30 - 3CCD MiniDV Camcorder with 60i and 30p modes, this camera was used to record the first two seasons of 'Ghost Hunters' before the switch to the HMC40 and subsequent switch to modified camcorders in recent seasons.

Pansonic AVCCAM HMC40 - 3CMOS Camcorder with AVCHD recording. The upgrade of the DVC30, the HMC40 was used to record several seasons of Ghost Hunters, Ghost Hunters Academy and Ghost Hunters International before being replaced by modified variants.

Ghost Adventures Camcorders

Sony HVR A1U - CMOS MiniDV Camcorder with 1080i and integrated audio mixer with XLR inputs. This camcorder was used several times in the first three seasons of Ghost Adventures.

Sony HDR FX7 - CMOS MiniDV Camcorder with 1080i, optional flash memory recording and integrated audio mixer with XLR inputs. This camcorder was used several times in the first three seasons of Ghost Adventures.

Sony HDR FX1000 - This CMOS MiniDV Camcorder with 1080i, flash memory and 24p record mode has been a staple of the Ghost Adventures arsenal throughout the series for its versatile nature.

Ghost Adventures Non-IR -

Sony HXR NX5U - First of the Sony NXCAM generation, AVCHD format, dual memory hybrid recording.

Sony PMW EX3 XDCAM EX HD -Flash-memory based high definition camcorder capable of a variety of frame rates and resolutions using Sony's new XDCAM-EX intraframe codec. A "big-brother" to the PMW-EX1, the PMW-EX3 ups the ante by providing an interchangeable lens mount. The Ghost Adventures team began using this camera in late 2011 for the documentary section of the show and is typically wielded only by Aaron Goodwin.

If you're wondering what Destination Truth, Fact or Faked or Ghost Hunters are using now, their Night Vision Camcorders are nothing but production camcorders with an adapter that allows them to attach a night vision monocle. This means that they only need one set of cameras and just replace the lenses with the IR scopes when they switch to night time shooting. They also use a wide array of low-light helmet cameras cabled to these camcorders to save the footage (watch the backpack shots at night).

When selecting a camcorder for IR purposes it is very important to remember that you'll probably want to use your camcorder for more than just its IR capabilities. This means you don't just want a dedicated camcorder for Ghost Hunting or IR shooting, unless you're feeling frivolous with expenses. This is where the prosumer camcorders like the Canon XA10 or Panasonic AGs would fit the bill (if you can find one cheap enough on eBay). Another option is to use an interchangeable lenses camcorder like the Destination Truth crew, although more cost efficient models like the Sony Nex VG10 or VG20H ($1,100.00-2,300.00). Saving money is a good thing when it comes to equipment but consider what that equipment may be used for when you're not poking around out at night. Sometimes it's better to spend well than be cheap in the long run.

Many have been asking what the POV cameras are that are used by Ghost Adventures, Ghost Hunters, Destination Truth,

Fact or Faked and the newest show to hit the roster Haunted Highway on Syfy.

Ghost Adventures use the 'Drift HD' Helmet Camera series as their "POV" cameras clipped on their shoulder. The GAC Crew used the Drift X170 as their first POV camera and have subsequently updated to the Drift Innovation HD170.

The Syfy Channel crews use the GoPro HD Hero2 Outdoor Ed helmet cameras. These are frequently seen mounted in the cars as the 'conversation camera' and used with slight modifications mounted to a swing support arm on the Destination Truth team in the field. Due to the narrow field of view at night these are always used as the personal camera aimed at the team member's face.

The new Syfy channel show Haunted Highway use the Sony HVR-A1U with a GoPro Camera facing the user so that the two cameras in use can also serve to record the investigator asking questions and reactions.

This makes the HVR-A1U quite a bit heavier by mounting a camera on a camera but also does well to replace the need for additional hands to shoot video from different angles.

Paranormal Central New York:

Through all of the paranormal investigations and reportedly haunted locations spread throughout Central New York one of the most interesting and stylish hauntings in the Mohawk Valley is the depression era Capitol Theater in Rome, NY.

Conceived by Michael and Joseph Kallet in 1926, the property at 216-224 West Dominick Street was purchased and the new theater was announced in December of 1926 but the theater was not confirmed until March of 1927 when construction began.

Originally planned for a Thanksgiving opening in 1928, a Pennsylvania steel strike delayed construction and prevented the theater from opening until December. Completed, the theater was designed as the premiere movie house in Rome with seating for 2,500, a Möller theater organ in the orchestra pit and two projectors designed for 'talking pictures."

In 1939 the theater received its Art Deco facelift but in 1974 the theater was closed as a 'first-run' movie house and shifted to theatrical productions and classic movies.

While there have been few tragic events over the last 83 years of operation, there have been a number of paranormal occurrences reported. The first reports date back more than thirty years to accounts of a ghostly figure in the balcony and phantom organ music despite the lack of a working organ until its repair in 2003.

Witnesses report the shadow figure of a man, which is believed to be a former projectionist. Others feel that it is the spirit of a performer that haunts the balcony and stage. There are also reports of a ghostly cat that stalks the theater. Organ music, whispered conversations, opening doors and even the sounds of plays have been experienced by those at the theater late at night.

Through all of the paranormal investigations and reportedly haunted locations spread throughout Central New York one of the most interesting and stylish hauntings in the Mohawk Valley is the depression era

Shadow Chasers Case Files:

Conceived by Michael and Joseph Kallet in 1926, the property at 216-224 West

Dominick Street was purchased and the new theater was announced in December of 1926 but the theater was not confirmed until March of 1927 when construction began.

In 1939 the theater received its Art Deco facelift but in 1974 the theater was closed as a 'first-run' movie house and shifted to theatrical productions and classic movies.

Originally planned for a Thanksgiving opening in 1928, a Pennsylvania steel strike delayed construction and prevented the theater from opening until December. Completed, the theater was designed as the premiere movie house in Rome with seating for 2,500, a Möller theater organ in the orchestra pit and two projectors designed for 'talking pictures."

While there have been few tragic events over the last 83 years of operation, there have been a number of paranormal occurrences reported. The first reports date back more than thirty years to accounts of a ghostly figure in the balcony and phantom organ music despite the lack of a working organ until its repair in 2003.

Witnesses report the shadow figure of a man, which is believed to be a former projectionist. Others feel that it is the spirit of a performer that haunts the balcony and stage. There are also reports of a ghostly cat that stalks the theater. Organ music, whispered conversations, opening doors and even the sounds of plays have been experienced by those at the theater late at night.

In the spring of 2010, the Shadow Chasers investigated the Rome Capitol Theater to document accounts of the hauntings at the site. The investigation started as the theater was closing up after the Saturday night movie.

The team divided into two teams to investigate the main auditorium sweeping for any anomalies. The primary anomalies were revealed as high EM from the aisle lighting from the seats. One peculiarity was a heightened EM field in the air above the ground floor seats.

Phil and Josh proceeded to investigate the dressing rooms under the stage while Kate and Courtinie moved to the concessions area to the second floor offices behind the balcony. While in the dressing room area Phil and Josh heard voices that they were able to record on camera. At the same time Kate and Courtinie heard voices coming from the stage area without any personnel visible.

Continuing the investigation into the maintenance tunnels Josh and Phil encountered a high energy field that drained all of the power from all of their electronics. As they started out of the tunnels to retrieve additional equipment they witnessed a ghostly cat that vanished into the prop-shop.

Kate and Courtinie were able to communicate with a spirit in the balcony through the use of a PX. The investigation concluded with the capture of a number of anomalous photos and EVPs.

In the spring of 2011 the team was requested back to conduct a ghost hunting training session for a number of individuals. This time the team divided into four separate teams of trainees. Kate and Courtinie led their teams to the balcony and the second floor offices while Josh led his team into the dressing room Phil was on the stage demonstrating the Full Spectrum (Para-Spectrum) Camera to his team when he snapped a burst series of the main auditorium.

A phantom figure appeared on the left staircase in one of the three shots while there were no individuals on the stairs at the time.

One of the trainees had the Vivitar night vision camera and was consistently taking pictures. Approximately a few moments after the Full Spectrum camera captured the phantom figure the trainee captured another phantom figure on the stairs to the balcony with no people in the frame.

The most startling event of the evening was actually at the conclusion to the night. Phil and his team were talking with the administrator of the Theatre on the second floor when everyone glimpsed a figure go into the front offices and slam the door. The administrator responded "Did you just see someone shut that door?" The nods from everyone in the group sent the administrator racing downstairs to come in through the front entrance to the second floor offices. When the administrator returned he had to unlock the door that everyone had witnessed a figure open and close. The administrator informed us that there was no plausible way for someone to open and close the door let-alone get out of the building without anyone noticing.

The hauntings of the Rome Capitol Theatre have proven that they are more than legends and rumors from the history of the location. Even with a large number of people on-site, the paranormal activity was frequent.

∞Paranormal Equipment∞

EMF Meters

One of the fundamentals of almost every investigative method for paranormal research is that of the radiological survey.

When it was first possible to measure environmental conditions, university researchers set about surveying a site for any possible environmental factor that could account for the paranormal phenomena and inadvertently identified a multitude of possible factors.

While there are a number of psychological factors that could account for reported paranormal phenomena, environmental scientists discovered even more potential causes including radiation.

Everything in the universe has an Electromagnetic Field or EMF. The Earth has a DC field called the 'Geomagnetosphere' that protects us from solar radiation. Artificial sources like power lines and electronics have larger AC fields. Even our bodies have a natural DC field (and an Electrostatic field) that are easily measurable. The affects of these fields and on these fields have led to much advancement in technology, but why would these have any effect on paranormal claims?

Radiations that can cause physiological and psychological alterations at a site consist of Electromagnetic Radiation (both AC and DC), Electrostatic, Radio Frequency and Ionizing radiation like Alpha, Beta, Gamma and X-Ray. All of these forms of radiation have a presence in modern environments and all can result in what is termed Electromagnetic Hypersensitivity or Electromagnetic Poisoning. It is this poisoning that can lead an unaware subject to believe that they are experiencing paranormal phenomena.

Electromagnetic Poisoning Symptoms:

- chronic fatigue
- daily headaches
- insomnia
- allergies
- high blood pressure
- brain fog
- ADD/ADHD
- migraine headaches
- lymphoblastic leukemia
- miscarriages
- stress
- nausea
- fatigue
- skin conditions – burning, rashes, pain
- tinnitus and other audible noises
- chronic pain
- erratic pulse
- weak immune system
- Hallucinations

These are just some of the symptoms that one can experience when subjected to excessive amounts of Electromagnetic Radiation. By identifying the radiation in the environment, it is possible to identify the potential sources of the "paranormal" activity. This is not to say all paranormal phenomena are simply excessive radiation but the large majority of studies have identified that what does not come from a routine source may be detectable as a radiological anomaly.

Identifying potential environmental radiation and radiological anomalies are environmental science at its finest. Physics scientists, environmental scientists, environmental geologists and environmental survey technicians study these fields and their effects every day. This is also where ghost hunters have adopted environmental survey techniques, the actual science that permits them to validate or invalidate claims from a scientific standpoint.

EMF Meters

Since ghost hunting and paranormal investigating hit the mainstream, everyone learns that you need an EMF Meter to hunt for ghosts. It's also at this point where skeptics jump up and say these devices do not detect ghosts, there is NO Science in what you are doing.

This is both true and false at the same time.

Knowing the effects electromagnetic radiation can have on a person gives a researcher something to measure for, something to look for in the environment. Through a radiological survey it is possible to scientifically identify with some certainty what 'could' be the cause of some accounts. It is also important to note that NO meter is capable of detecting ghosts. Anomalies identified through a survey are just that, radiological anomalies.

If an EMF meter is used properly, then it is possible to identify potential sources and any anomalies that are within the environment.

EMF Meter vs. EMF Detector

Nothing is more frustrating as a researcher than having amateur ghost hunters and would-be researchers referring to their technology based on what they've learned from TV shows. If you want to be taken seriously as a researcher, learn the science.

EMF Meter - An EMF meter is any radiological survey device that 'measures' and provides some means of identifying field strength intensity.

EMF Detector - An EMF Detector is any radiological survey device that can 'identify' a field and indicate the basic intensity (not a measured strength).

Many individuals always tend to argue their point both about this and the term 'debunk' but always fail to see the point. Anyone that wants to hold their work as credible strives to provide little ammunition for skeptics. Failing to understand professional terminology is the first step toward discrediting your work for any skeptic.

EMF Meter Usage

Using an EMF meter properly, or any radiological survey device for that matter, is greatly dependant on understanding the capabilities of the device, the specifications and the intended usage.

For instance, the most common device is the Lutron 822-A EMF meter. This device measures on a single axis across the 30 - 400hz AC field and is designed to measure accurately 50/60hz range in either Milligauss or MicroTesla with accuracy of 4% at that range. This means it is the most accurate when measuring AC or artificial fields and loses accuracy depending on the frequency above and below that intended usage. Single Axis also means that the meter needs to be rotated to measure on all 3 Axis.

Depending on the model, a survey meter may measure on multiple axis or it may require you to manually rotate to measure for the peak field strength.

DC EMF meters work on a very similar principle and scale however; most of these devices are subject to interference from other natural fields within the environment. These require extensive training and time to use properly to survey a site.

Another device may be an electrostatic monitor or an Air Ion counter. These measure ions as parts-per-millionth (ppm) and determine the calculated micro voltage. There are no axis to measure with these as they measure by contact with a field.

Still, another type of meter may measure for classic radiation like Alpha, Beta, Gamma or X-Rays and in many instances these devices are limited in which 'band' they are measuring for in the field. The more fields that a radiological meter measures, the more the accuracy of those measurements decrease.

Capacitor Circuit vs. Magnetometer

The two most prominent types of devices in paranormal research at the moment are based on one of two types of technology, either a capacitive circuit or a magnetomer.

Capacitive Circuit - A capacitor circuit measures the change in the field of the capacitor as the energy moves the field on the electroplate. Many 'detectors' including the K-2, K II 'meters' use a capacitive circuit. The downside is that capacitive circuits can be influenced by any field effectively invalidating any results.

Magnetometer - A magnetometer circuit comes in one of three forms; Vector, Ring Core, and Search Coil sensors. The principle is a sensitive metal is pulled in a direction and the pull is measured to determine field strength. These are ALL EMF meters. This means that any sudden movement can cause changes in readings and if the motion is strong enough it could cause calibration issues.

Survey - A survey is conducted by holding the survey meter approximately 20inches from the body, stopping every 3-5ft and slowly moving in sweeping motions before advancing. If it is single axis or dual-axis it may require you to rotate the meter as you 'sweep.' Once a peak is identified that measurement it then followed to identify its source.

It is very important to note that most hand-held meters suffer from accuracy issues and may produce different results when surveying a site multiple times. External factors like electricity pulses in the lines, saturation of the meter's circuits and even weather conditions can affect the accuracy of these devices. If you're measuring for AC EMF fields, Electrostatic or RF there are countless contamination sources that could throw-off measurements and accuracy during a survey. Even additional electronics in hand can affect a sensor decreasing the accuracy of your survey.

Geophysicists utilize magnetometers routinely, and to assure their accuracy these devices are quite large. They consist of a 20-30lb backpack array, a tablet computer and a large sensor that is on a pole 5-6ft off the ground to prevent contamination. Surveys are conducted by stopping to take readings every 3-6ft in a grid-like pattern. You may have a handheld unit but just remember accuracy is an issue with those units.

Flashy Ghost Hunting

The most scientific part of ghost hunting is the environmental survey, but many regard it with awe when the ghost hunter takes out that unusual looking device with all of the blinking lights. To the lay-person this is the most interesting part of ghost hunting and to a degree it's what ghost hunters like as well. In all honesty, every paranormal investigator wants their own version of a proton pack.

In reality, conducting a site survey with EMF meters and other radiological survey meters is a very dull and laborious process.

- You establish a 'baseline' for the site and make note of what would be a variation over or below that measurement.

- You systematically divide up the site, thinking of the layout in a grid.
- You follow that grid tracing readings within that space.
- You do not immediately measure electronics based on assumptions. (Accurate measurements will guide you to the source within that space).
- Decrease the interference with the survey by reducing potential radiation sources. (i.e. electronics on your person, contamination sources like wifi, radios etc.)
- Any fields that cannot have a source identified are noted as anomalies.

Following this basic survey method will assure the most accurate results and validate potential EMF Poisoning sources. Sadly, this is also where amateur ghost hunters can fail miserably by invalidating their own results in favor of flash.

The Proton Pack Approach

A lot of investigators want to have something flashy, their own proton pack or they just want to minimize their time spent doing a survey. So, these investigators will resort to carrying multiple electronics while conducting a survey or they will combine electronics into one device this effectively invalidates any readings with the device.

Quite often, creative investigators will take kids toys like the Eyclops Night Vision goggles and add an EMF meter to it (in this case an electro-sensor) to simplify the survey and make it 'flash.' The accuracy of the EMF meter is already questionable and adding electronics to it only assures that the device will never accurately measure.

Any readings taken when devices are combined like the eyclops/electrosensor or the camcorder/electrosensor are open to skeptics to discredit because of the inaccuracies of those readings.

If you are attempting a scientific approach to your ghost hunting, then it is necessary to understand your technology, as well as the methods and techniques required. It is very dull but you will have valid data. If you're after your own proton pack-style then expect skeptics to discredit your methods immediately. You are using a kid's toy after-all.

Finally, if the dry radiological survey doesn't sound like your style then you may want to consider a different method altogether, maybe a documentarian?

I originally started formally investigating the paranormal back in 2001/2002 as the result of an anthropology fieldwork course. When I was first starting out it was a matter of anthropology- claims of the paranormal were just folkloric accounts. All I needed was a cassette recorder to document the accounts and access to a computer to transcribe the interview for the records. Investigations were simple and the purpose was clear, document the folklore to preserve these legends.

In late 2002-2003, investigations took on another aspect, understanding why people believed in these stories. Adding environmental survey technology and even psychology to investigations became the norm. Environmental survey tech was needed to authenticate claims, was there something in the environment that was causing behavioral changes or was there objective evidence to be found?

Since that time, investigations became a combination of authentication technology and documentation technology. At first it was magnetometers and hardline CTS cameras but things were still in question. Investigations were laborious and the technology was only adding to the problem. To assure that the client was receiving the best possible results we had to keep appraised of new technology that could help and adopt whatever was best for our work.

Today paranormal investigation technology still falls into one of three primary categories/roles; Documentation, Authentication and Communication/Experimental.

The best possible technology for any paranormal investigation or ghost hunt currently available includes:

Documentation

- Sony HDD Nightshot Camcorders for portability and extended-life batteries with slow-shot & tripods for static cams. These make setting up a quick effort and are far more adaptable than hardline or wireless CTS camera systems.
- Zoom H1/H3 Audio Recorders for clarity of audio and sophistication of playback capabilities.

Authentication

- Magnitec 263 Tri-field AC Electromagnetic Radiation meter. This EMF meter is the most accurate providing peak axis and RMS averaging with adjustable backlit display.
- Archos 5 IMT This tablet is easily adaptable becoming an EMF meter, oscilloscope, RF analyzer or anything else that could be necessary depending on the accessories available.

Communication/Experimental

- PX Ovilus from Digital Dowsing. The device takes in environmental energies and outputs the results as audible translations such as phonetics or samples from the internal dictionary.

New Ghost Hunting Technology

While these are the best possible technology for ghost hunting right now it doesn't meant that there aren't new innovations in the works. Through our experience we have found many questionable technology sources and a few very strong, reliable sources. Amazon and eBay are very strong places for finding technology if you know what you are looking for but these are not the newest tech, nor the most innovative. The best technology outfitters that we have found include LessEMF, Digital Dowsing, Paranologies and Ghoststop.

One innovation in camera technology is the new Looxcie LX2 camcorder. This is an ear-worn 5-10hr camcorder that utilizes Bluetooth technology to pair with a Smartphone or tablet. The Looxcie is designed to record at standard resolution for a set period of time or the most innovative feature; record on a continuous loop at lower quality and saving short clips as the record button is pressed. While not an IR camera it makes an excellent POV cam with wireless capabilities so it can be viewed from 15-20ft away.

Digital Dowsing and founder Bill Chapel are widely known for his creative innovations in ghost hunting technology. Digital Dowsing has a wide array of innovative and brilliant technology with both soft-science and legitimate science for paranormal authentication.

Some of the most brilliant technologies that have recently been developed include the Thermasound, a device that scans a room for sonar and thermal variations logging multiple data points that can later be reviewed; The Visual Ovilus, basically an IR camera with a built-in ovilus that displays the words on the video; the ES Probe, a device that translates audio impulses into electromagnetic impulses; the SEM detectors, an E-detector that reacts to bio-electric, DC, AC and static fields.

Ghoststop has become a large ghost hunting outfitter and is not only responsible for all of the basic investigative tools but they have also started producing a few new devices including a new long-life laser net for more accurate measurements and an experimental spirit touch device that is similar in design to the SEM detectors built by Digital Dowsing.

This new technology is not entirely innovative but they do have improvements on basic equipment and a wide array drawing on the most practical and widely used ghost hunting technology by amateur investigators.

The most innovative new technology that we have seen is actually coming from custom designers that have extensive experience with electronics and ghost hunting. Groups like Moditronic that modify cameras and produce Full Spectrum Cameras (or Para-spectrum) that video and photo UV and IR, or produce devices like the Paracorder, a static detector and EM pump. Other individuals manufacture Geophones, EM pumps and IR illuminators to help with authentication or documentation of phenomena.

One group that is producing the most innovative new paranormal technology is Paranologies. A group out of Texas that is producing the most creative and professional technology to fill the gaps in current ghost hunting technology with devices like 180 illuminators (UV, IR) that light up a full room; Parascope, a simple energy detectors (like digital dowsing); Para-Pyramid that provides sonar detection; more sophisticated geophones; integrated dvr 180 cameras and by-far the most brilliant piece of technology the Tri-Field Audio-Visual Recorder, a device that films 4 different angles at once with two independent channel Omni-directional microphones.

In the past, paranormal research equipment has been developed in laboratories for university researchers. As ghost hunting became a mainstream past-time, the last decade has seen more innovation in authentication, documentation and communication technology than any other point in research history. One can only wonder what the next advancements will be.

Paranormal Central New York

In 1918, World War I was raging, and any company that was able to be adapted to a military need was eager to. One such company was the Solvay Process Company in Syracuse. They owned a limestone quarry outside of Syracuse in the town of Onondaga, and were willing to convert this quarry into a munitions factory to help the war effort. This quarry was known as the Split Rock Quarry.

On July 2, 1918, due to a machinery malfunction a fire broke out within the factory. The fire was unable to be stopped, and spread to the flammable chemicals stored within the building. This led to a massive explosion that dest   `he factory, as well as damaging nearby build'   ~e to 50 people lost their lives in th

This explosion did nr
explosives at the munitior
remain operative throur
was later used as a r
York State Departr
was abandoned

The tragic past of the Split Rock Quarry continues to make its presence known. Even though the quarry has been closed for close to 20 years, it is the site of regular paranormal investigations. Documented sightings have been of strange green and blue lights, as well as seeing apparitions of those killed during the explosion. Many attribute the strange coloration of the apparitions witnessed to those who were killed by pyric acid when the explosion occurred.

Shadow Chasers Case Files

On June 2nd, the Shadow Chasers travelled to Syracuse to investigate the reportedly haunted Split Rock Quarry in Syracuse, New York.

Planning Phase:

In most investigations you contact the proprietor and work with them to set up an ideal investigation date. The Split Rock Quarry was quite a bit different. Despite the countless reports of investigations that have taken place at the location and the number of blogs that report Split Rock Quarry is a great place to go hiking or biking, there is relatively no information about the state of the location or how one can visit the site. All of the information we could attain were a few blogs and an article from a Syracuse newspaper about a local ghost hunting team that had investigated the site and our own CNY Paranormal article about the legends.

In the end all we had was a rough location and a Google map with what looked to be the site at the end of a road.

Road Trip:

We set out for Syracuse before noon and met up with our team member Sean for lunch at Kelley's Bar and Grill just a short 15min from the quarry according to the gps. We discussed the history of the location and all of the reported activity from the site.

Investigations by local teams all claimed extensive history and activity on the site. We arrived at the entrance to Split Rock Quarry after 1PM.

To our dismay we encountered a rather large barricade to the entrance and warning against parking. Since we were were in unfamiliar territory, we discussed our options. We were on the dead end of a neighborhood road with no potential locations to park except in residents driveways. The parking issue was not our only issue as this barricade meant that any equipment that we were to take would have to be portable.

Fortunately, some residents were rather helpful and offered us advice about parking and how far the main quarry was from our entrance. After dealing with the parking issue, and under the threat of getting our cars towed, we headed up the entrance driveway to Split Rock Quarry. Climbing the steadily increasing incline we finally arrived at the leveled area of the quarry.

Unlike other quarries, Split Rock Quarry was actually elevated and carved into the hillside. We were greeted with a steep embankment on our right and a sharp rise on our left but it wasn't until we cleared the foliage that we could see the Rock crusher for the first time.

On Site:

As we walked up to the famous 'Rock Crusher' of Split Rock Quarry we discovered just how massive and popular the structure was. A number of teens were climbing on the exterior of the structure. The Rock Crusher itself was a giant step pyramid carved back into the hillside. According to blogs and accounts, the Rock crusher was host to a series of labyrinthine tunnels and caves that webbed throughout the site. our research showed at least two tunnels that seemed to be on either side of the main structure.

The "Rock Crusher" was also our first encounter with the inaccuracies of the legends and accounts from Split Rock Quarry. There were indeed two tunnels on either side of the main structure. We were uncertain of what we might encounter upon entering the structure and quickly discovered what this 'web of tunnels' really was.

The two tunnels traveled back about 60 feet in a straight flat path and meet with a back wall of sorts where the two tunnels merge and follow a slightly circular arc along the hillside until emerging only a couple hundred yards from the first tunnel entrance. This was hardly a 'web of tunnels.' Throughout the tunnel there were huge piles of debris and refuse with slight traces of the explosion that devastated the property over 100 years earlier.

Investigation:

We opened our investigation by first climbing the exterior of the "Rock Crusher" to gather some sense of the area and identify any other potentially interesting areas that we may not have been able to see. This was an extremely dangerous and somewhat effective task as the exterior of the rock crusher is little more than giant stone steps, but like the pyramids it does rise significantly in height and the contours of the rock change with height. Our survey identified several areas that looked interesting further off to our left across the quarry.

After the teens left the area we set a number of recorders and cameras to record throughout the "Rock Crusher" and we left the equipment to record while we headed out across the site to continue our survey. Once more, despite the numerous stories, we discovered there was little else of interest aside from an alarming number of shotgun shells scattered throughout the site.

There really wasn't much else throughout the site aside from more debris that had been dumped at the site recently and literally thousands of shotgun shells and a few ATV trails.

This brought us back to the "Rock Crusher" where we conducted our investigation. Upon returning to the site, Sean witnessed a man in an orange jacket atop the hillside next to the 'Rock Crusher', where the figure mysteriously vanished. Josh, following the hilltop path, did not see the figure.

After all of the team reunited at the "Rock Crusher" we checked the equipment and added a few pieces of gear to the site monitoring including a new IR sensor that Sean had created.

The remainder of the investigation continued without incident aside from the occasional couple of hikers that were visiting the site. Every couple of hours another couple would come to the quarry to walk with their dogs.

The Wrap Up:

Our investigation of Split Rock Quarry concluded with a bit of a thunderstorm and rain that encouraged us to expedite packing and hike back to the cars. On our hike back we discussed how remote the location was, the number of shotgun shells and the fact that there were graffiti tags throughout the site. The Shadow Chasers investigation of Split Rock Quarry was certainly an adventure. We captured a number of audible phenomena on multiple cameras and audio recorders. We captured a few interesting photographs and had a number of experiences. Would we want to go back and investigate the quarry again? No.

The legends and folklore of the site far exceed the activity of the site. While there are indicators that the site is active, the perils and contamination of the site prevent it from being a verifiable or desirable location to investigate. The thousands of shotgun shells indicate people use the area for a shooting range routinely and the hazards of the site (drop offs, rusted metal, crumbling stone work) certainly discourage exploration.

The Split Rock Quarry is known for its history and for its accounts of paranormal activity. The site is historic and holds a tragic past, but there is little activity to justify the perils of the site. It is difficult to get to, hazardous to explore and those ambitious enough to follow the legends may just end up adding to the site's history if they are not careful.

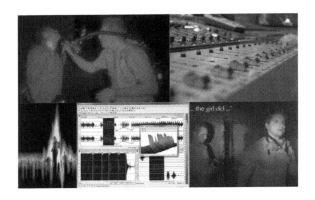

∞Evaluating the Evidence∞

Evidence Analysis:

When it comes to investigating the paranormal, historical research, technology and even conducting the investigation are only a small portion of the actual work. The most significant portion of work in paranormal investigating is the actual evaluation of the evidence and presenting it to the client.

Evidence analysis typically takes hours or even days depending on the amount of video footage, audio and photos that were taken during the course of the paranormal investigation. A simple example of this would be a basic investigation that utilizes 6 static cameras, 4 hand-held cameras, 4 voice recorders and

2 still cameras. If the investigation takes 8 hours, then that can equal 80 hours of video, 32 hours of audio and several hundred photos just for a one night investigation. The analysis of this data can take three people up to 12 hours to review or more.

The burdensome task of conveying these results to the client can be accomplished in a simple presentation, but if you're attempting to convey the validity of your work, a couple of digital files and what the client remembers of what you told them does not help.

Typically a client expects copies of any evidence that you obtain and some explanation for the results of your investigation. The extensive results need to be explained in some fashion that can be interpreted by other investigators that follow in your footsteps because at its heart, science is about replicating tests to duplicate results. If another investigator cannot duplicate your tests then your results are inherently flawed.

This is why many professional teams present their evidence in the form of a written report that can be easily interpreted by the client or other investigators. The elements of these reports vary widely but include three primary areas; the team experiences, media evidence and survey.

When the Shadow Chasers were first created, it was a matter of anthropological research combined with environmental survey methods, so it was only natural to present data to the client in the form of an environmental survey report with an anthropological summary of the investigation.

This approach was fine for a number of years, It provided perfectly accurate information that any investigator could follow after our investigation. It was also presented in a professional scientific manner that demonstrated our level of professionalism in the field. Unfortunately, most clients were only interested in a summary and the evidence. Worse still, few clients could interpret the scientific jargon and presentation. It also took us a number of days to compile the data into the report and some reports were in excess of 9 pages.

It was apparent that our reporting process was flawed and needed to be changed to something that the client was interested in and could understand. It needed to be simplified.

After some discussion and retooling, the reports that we presented to the client needed to have 3 primary aspects; a summary of the results, a discussion of the site and investigation methods and a summary of the evidence found in each of the categories: Experiences, Photo, Video and Audio. We allowed the summary of methods and protocol to be shortened into a simple summary that could point back to other documents rather than be forced into the report, and used abbreviated summaries for each of the smaller sections. The reports were compressed to exactly what the client was looking for and nothing more but still had all of the scientific data referenced so that it could be validated.

Reporting and evidence presentation are a fundamental requirement for paranormal research in order to establish credibility and validity. It's not only about how you conduct the investigation it's about what the client needs and what they will have as an example of your work.

It is very common while researching the paranormal to get caught up in reports and accounts of the ghostly activity and lose perspective. The history of a site is not limited to the structure or immediate grounds. Often significant historical events can affect an entire region to leave multiple locations and artifacts with potential hauntings.

A renowned example of a historic event causing regional activity is the Battle of Gettysburg. A sustained event over the course of several days has resulted in countless reports of paranormal activity spread through multiple locations, objects and individuals. In Central New York we have many variations of these regions but none so clearly defined as Herkimer.

Paranormal Central New York:

While Herkimer was established in the early 1700s some events have established the "Historic Four Corners" as one of the most haunted regions in the Mohawk Valley. The Four Corners are a series of buildings built at approximately the same time and consist of Suiter Building Museum, Herkimer County Jail, Herkimer County Courthouse, and the Herkimer Reformed Church. In the 1880s Roxalana Druce brutally murdered her husband after his abuse became too much. She was incarcerated at the Herkimer Jail, tried at the Old Herkimer Courthouse and hung. Her rocking chair is now one of the featured exhibition pieces at the Suiter Building Museum. In 1907 Chester Gillette was placed on trial for the murder of Grace Brown, incarcerated at the jail, tried at the courthouse and sentenced to death in Auburn. These are just a few of events that have tied the buildings together over the years.

While there are countless legends about the hauntings of the Herkimer Jail there are more actual reports of ghostly activity from the surrounding four corners buildings associated with Druce and Gillette trials ranging from Chester Gillette's Attorney wandering the halls of the courthouse to Roxalana's rocking chair rocking by itself. When there is an event significant enough to cause a haunting it does not mean that it is restricted to the site. Historical events can affect entire regions.

Shadow Chasers Case Files:

Recently, the Shadow Chasers investigated the Eckler, Suiter and Courthouse buildings on-behalf of the Herkimer Historical Society. While the historical society was uncertain of any results that would be obtained from the Eckler and especially the Suiter building, since it was never a residence, they were surprised by the results.

While the Suiter Building was never a residence it was an active doctor's office and it was where autopsies were performed for cases that were going to trial next door at the courthouse. The doctor's testimony was imperative to the Herkimer Court especially in the Roxalana Druce and Chester Gillette trials. The results from this investigation included a number of EVPs that could be associated with the trials as well as one of a small child that reacted to one of the static cameras.

The Herkimer Courthouse was a paramount case with legends of apparitions that stalked the courtroom re-enacting the Grace Brown murder committed by Chester Gillette. While the courthouse is still in-use by the Herkimer County Sheriff's Department, the accounts of haunting activity still abounds. Personal Accounts from deputies and court-workers include seeing the apparition of Chester Gillette's attorney walking the halls, moving objects, phantom footsteps and even the sounds of a trial replaying in the courtroom.

During the investigation we managed to capture a fleeting figure in a photo but more importantly in addition to a number of EVPs of voices and even what sound like the sounds of a trial we managed to capture the reported shadow apparition in the courtroom that walks from chamber doors to the judges' bench before turning back and quickly 'folding down and away.'

∞Psychology of the Paranormal∞

So you think your house is haunted? The first thing to do is not to panic. We receive a lot of contacts from people upset or frightened because they feel that their house is haunted, and want whatever is there gone.

It is normal to be scared about things that we don't understand, and can't see, especially when there is no prior experience with the paranormal. We try and inform everyone that we encounter, especially those struggling with the paranormal in their own home, that they have nothing to be scared of when encountering spirits. However, in the middle of the night, when they are hearing thumping noises, it is hard to accept that fact.

Which brings us back to the first point- do not panic. When you start to panic, you stop thinking clearly, and are unable to analyze the situation thoroughly.

A common result of paranormal investigations is that natural causes are in effect. There is usually some environmental factor in effect. This can be as simple as a loose shutter causing a banging noise, or malfunctioning wiring or a furnace. Before panicking about having a haunted house, take a look around the house and check to make sure if everything is operating properly.

When we are contacted by a client upset by the paranormal in their home and unable to get into the house immediately, we suggest a number of techniques to help manage the situation in the home until we can get there. These are temporary solutions, and are not designed to be permanent. They are simple to implement, and are designed to provide temporary relief.

The first thing that we suggest is the usage of a humidifier in the house. The higher the humidity in the house, the harder it is for paranormal activity to occur. This is easy for the homeowner to accomplish, and has a quick effect.

Second, we suggest burning incense. We conduct cleansings when requested by homeowners, but it is beneficial to leave a stick or two of incense burning in the home. This helps clean out some of the negative energy in the home prior to our arrival.

After we have conducted the investigation, there are a couple options that we try. The Shadow Chasers emphasize the importance of communication with spirits, and will try to communicate with the spirits the level of discomfort the homeowners are having, and try and work out a solution to the problem that way. We also talk with the homeowners about what we have discovered about the spirits in their home. We have found that having knowledge about the spirits in their home is helpful in encouraging homeowners to accept that their house is haunted, and coexist in peace with their spirits.

If this method does not work, we make every effort to remediate the situation, utilizing the strategies mentioned at the beginning of the chapter as well as conducting a cleansing of the house to remove negative energy.

The important thing to keep in mind when you feel that you have a haunted house is to remember that the spirits are deceased people, and are not trying to act scary or aggressive. They have found themselves in an unfamiliar situation. They are a stranger in their own home, invisible and unheard, adjusting to the lack of a physical form. Spirits are rarely mean and aggressive. They are just unsure of how to interact with their environment, and may utilize more force than is necessary. So, don't panic.

Paranormal Central New York:

Turning historic homes into Bed and Breakfasts has become increasingly popular in our society. Older homes change owners so frequently that it is rare to find a home that has remained in one family throughout its existence. In some of these Bed and Breakfasts, those former owners remain, even beyond the grave…

The Collinwood Inn in Oneida NY is currently a Bed and Breakfast with an interesting theme. The Victorian mansion's rooms are decorated in a Dark Shadows theme, a popular '60s soap opera featuring plenty of vampires and ghosts. While the Gothic theme of the show compliments the classic Victorian woodwork, the location has an even closer tie to the supernatural theme. The Collinwood Inn is host to multiple deceased guests, most of them tied to the long history of the home, and the antiques that decorate it.

The Collinwood was build in the late 1860s by Stephen Farnam, a local business owner and respected citizen of Oneida. Stephen passed away in the home, as did two of his sons. It is believed that Stephen, and his son, Fred, continue to reside in the home they loved.

Two other residents of the home also passed away in the home, and are believed to remain there to this day.

Activity at the Collinwood Inn consists of lights turning on and off, voices, and strange shadows appearing in photographs. Multiple guests have reported odd occurrences. Most interestingly, there is an old clock in the séance room of the Collinwood that makes it known when it needs to be wound. There have been sightings of a spirit standing next to the clock when it is in need of a winding. Once the clock is wound, there are no more sightings of the spirit until the next time the clock starts running down.

Some Bed and Breakfasts choose to ignore the haunted history of their home, fearful that it scares away potential visitors. Others, like the Collinwood Inn, choose to embrace their hauntings as part of their unique history.

Shadow Chasers Case Files:

The brick Italianate Victorian mansion that is now the Collinwood Inn was built sometime between 1865 and 1870 for Stephen H. Farnam, a successful business owner, President of the National State Bank, and President of the Glenwood Cemetery Association. He was also one of the organizers and first directors of the Oneida Gas Light Company and served on its board of directors until his death. Stephen H. Farnam, who was for many years a well-known and highly esteemed citizen of Oneida, died in his home on November 17, 1897. According to his obituary, the cause of death was apoplexy. His funeral took place from the Farnam Mansion and his body was interred in Oneida's Glenwood Cemetery, which is known for having some of the grandest and most unusual tombstones in Upstate New York.

Over the years the mansion has been home to a number of people from many different walks of life. In the early 1900s it was owned by a locally famous woman by the name of Mary Dyer Jackson. An early activist in the women's suffrage movement, she was the first woman to circulate a petition in Central New York for the women's suffrage cause. She also founded the Progress Club in 1889 and became a charter member of the Madison County Historical Society in 1898..

The next owner of the house was Dr. Robert L. Crockett, who specialized in ailments of the eyes, ears, nose and throat. Dr. Crockett was Mayor of Oneida from 1916-1917 before leaving to serve in World War I. An amateur botanist, the good doctor had a laboratory in the basement of the mansion, and it was there that he suffered a fatal heart attack on May 27, 1946. His widow sold the mansion to Dr. Chancellor Whiting in 1952, who in turn sold it to another doctor ten years later. Dr. William Hummer, the last doctor to own the mansion, died in his bedroom. The cause of death was colon cancer. His death came almost two years after the death of his wife. Her lifeless body was found in one of the small parlors on the mansion's first floor, which is currently used as a bedroom.

Not surprisingly, some guests of the Collinwood Inn have reported strange unexplained phenomena while staying there, ranging from phantom cats in their rooms to lights turning on and off by themselves. Other people have witnessed apparitions, shadow figures, ghostly voices, and strange sounds and sensations. Many who have experienced these things are convinced that the spirits of those who have died in the Farnam Mansion have never left the house.

The Shadow Chasers investigated the Farnam Mansion on-behalf of the proprietors Gerri and Brian. While they were curious what the team would actually be able to document they were certain that we would be able to capture something.

While the Farnam Mansion had a very interesting history the team had to approach the site objectively. Gerri and Brian gave a guided tour of the mansion explaining in great detail all of the history that they had uncovered about the site. The unique aspect that we discerned from the proprietors was that while the theme of the mansion had been shifted to emulate the Dark Shadows TV show from the late 1960s, the entirety of the mansion had been painstakingly restored to its relatively original condition with antique furniture.

The investigation of the Farnam Mansion started off rather interestingly. As the team split up and set about establishing the baseline data for the site, Josh and Phil remained on the first floor while everyone else proceeded to the basement. Before they could even establish a baseline they witnessed a shadow figure dart along the exterior wall in the front parlor and activate the lamp in the room. When they moved to investigate they heard footsteps and voices coming from the room directly above them on the second floor. Investigating these phenomena confirmed that there was no possible source.

During the investigation on the second floor we caught a light anomaly that darted around the corner of a doorway and footsteps from the attic. While investigating the attic we witnessed shadow figures moving at the periphery of the attic, catching a number of orb phenomena.

After meeting with the rest of the team on the second floor, we proceeded to test the ITC equipment and were promptly shocked by the results on the stairs. The PX device responded with highly accurate information regarding a female spirit and the surrounding antiques in the house.

Shifting to investigating the basement we were able to communicate with a spirit through ITC equipment, the spirit was dubbed 'Fred' and gave intelligent responses on the PX and through the voice recorders. After a thirty-minute conversation with the spirit through the electronics we slowly began wrapping up the investigation. It was clear before we even began putting away the equipment that the Farnam Mansion was haunted and the spirits were very happy to communicate.

Working with the Farnam Mansion, the Shadow Chasers put together the first ever Night of

Shadows to help educate the public about ghost hunting and the history of the site. The night was even more active than the investigation as participants were able to experience the footsteps, phantom voices and shadow apparitions first hand. At midnight the proprietors conducted a Victorian Séance in the front Séance Room with everyone in the room. The activity in the mansion increased to the point of heavy footsteps pacing the halls and even the apparition of a cat appearing.

Paranormal Central New York:

One of the questions paranormal investigators ask themselves is regarding the location of haunted sites. Anecdotal evidence tells us that there are a lot of haunted buildings by rivers and other bodies of water. Folklore tells us that ghosts can't cross running water, so does this mean that spirits hit a river and then stop at the nearest building? Science tells us that water conducts electricity dissipating the current, so it is a barrier to the passage of electricity, which backs up the folklore. That still leaves us with the question about hauntings near bodies of water. Whether you believe in science or folklore, we are left with a lot of ghosts residing along our waterways.

One Central New York location that follows this haunted waterways trend is the Stone Mill of Little Falls, located along the canal in Little Falls NY. Built in 1839, this building was initially used as a textile mill, creating cloth for the Mexican-American War and the Civil War. Over the years, and with slight expansions to the business, World War II uniforms were also produced in this building. Currently, the Stone Mill of Little Falls is home to a number of businesses ranging from an antiques store, to an ice cream store. Additionally, there are professional offices located in the building, as well as an Inn located on the third floor.

The Stone Mill of Little Falls has a history of haunted happenings. From spotting of shadow figures to lights turning on and off, the Stone Mill is a prime example of a haunted waterway building. There have been multiple reports of full-bodied apparitions in various locations in the building. A man believed to be a firefighter has been spotted in one of the downstairs shops, as well as on a staircase. A ghostly audience member has been spotted in the Black Box Theater on the second floor of the building. These paranormal experiences don't cover the other paranormal reports of footsteps, ghostly voices, and strange photographs.

Whatever the reason for haunted waterways, there is no question about the haunting at the Stone Mill. When visiting this historic location, be sure to keep your eyes open for ghostly visitors.

Hauntings on the Rails

When investigating the paranormal over the years it has become apparent that there are certain types of sites that are more prone to being labeled as haunted regardless of their actual history. Places like old theaters, cemeteries, schools and so forth. Then there are places that not only are hazardous locations but often have tragic histories.

There are many daily locations that have numerous tragic events but none as strongly as the railways and railroad stations. All over the world there are accounts of paranormal phenomena associated with the tragedies on the railway lines. The most common accounts are of the 'ghost-light' along the tracks at night, the ghost of a conductor walking the tracks, the spirits of children pushing stalled cars over the tracks, passengers haunting the stations and even ghostly porters or conductors haunting the passenger cars of old trains.

Union Station in Utica is no stranger to tragedy. Originally constructed in mid-1800, the station has been reported to have ghostly passengers and conductors moving about in the late-night hours. One of the most notable tragedies occurred in August of 1844 when a passenger train left the station and ran into mechanical difficulties. As the train was stopped on the tracks for repairs, a freight train unaware of the stopped train collided with the passenger train killing a conductor and a 12-year-old 'Irish Immigrant' girl. Over the years there have been hundreds of incidents along the railways both at the station and the surrounding smaller stations like the Remsen Depot.

There are numerous accounts of bystanders and even passenger cars being struck by passing trains on the rural railways surrounding the larger stations due to lack of warning or more often just misfortunate timing. The most common haunting reports from places like the Remsen Depot are not associated with the tragedies but the emotions that these places represent. Railway stations are places where people are very emotional, they are saying goodbye, they're ecstatic that someone is arriving or they're afraid as they're starting a new life in a new town. These emotions are responsible for many of the late-night ghostly accounts at the stations. Reports of feeling watched in the station, the ghostly figures walking the grounds or the vanishing conductor that greets would-be passengers as they enter the station.

There are more than 280 reported railway disasters in New York since the early 1800's with thousands of deaths and injuries over the thousands of miles of railway lines. Every railway station, each train and section of track has numerous accounts of ghostly activities.

Historic Ghosts:

The Hulbert House was built in 1812 in Boonville, NY. Since it was built, Hulbert House has been active as an inn, and was at one time one of the most well-known places to stay in the region. Their registration book holds the signatures of many historic figures- including Ulysses S. Grant, 18th President of the United States.

Hulbert House is also well-known for guests of another type, the spirits of those connected with the site while living. Hulbert House has been investigated by many local paranormal teams, and all have obtained fairly consistent information. Most notably, Hulbert House is scheduled to appear on SyFy's Haunted Collector.

Paranormal activity that has been observed includes a man who is referred to as 'Wayne'. He appears as a large man in a Civil War uniform. He has appeared in the bar, and is heard walking around the second floor. Children have been heard playing upstairs in the hotel area, and the image of a small girl was captured in a photograph taken during a paranormal investigation.

The Shadow Chasers had an opportunity to investigate Hulbert House as part of a fundraiser associated with our Haunted History Investigations. In addition to strange energy readings, we encountered the spirit of an older woman on the third floor who interacted with those present, as well as a man on the second floor who made noises in response to investigators.

The more historic and tragic a site, the more common it is to find legends of its hauntings. While there are many historic sites with a tragic history it seems that it is even more common to find rumors of hauntings associated with a historic site because a significant historic figure came to that location at one point.

The association of a historical figure with that site immediately stirs to consciousness that the individual may be haunting that site. This brings the history alive for many today. A renowned example of this thinking is the historic figure Thomas Jefferson, who drafted the Declaration of Independence, founded Virginia College, and built Monticello to name a few amazing feats. Today people claim to encounter his ghost everywhere from Constitution Hall in Pennsylvania to Boston to his former estate of Monticello.

In Central New York General Nicholas Herkimer experiences a similar stature. His career began during the French and Indian War as he assisted in the defense of German Flatts and was subsequently made captain in the militia in 1758. It wasn't until 1777 with the siege of Fort Stanwix did General Herkimer find one of the most influential moments in Colonial New York. Herkimer led the

Tryon County Militia on a march from Fort Dayton to save Fort Stanwix and were ambushed by a force of British Regulars at what is now know as the Battle of Oriskany. Herkimer was wounded at the battle and despite his wound he kept command of his troops to prevent further losses. He was brought back to Herkimer Home where he died from an amateur amputation.

Today people report witnessing his ghost at German Flatts, Fort Dayton, the Oriskany Battlefield and his home in Little Falls. While many credit Herkimer himself for haunting the Herkimer Home State Site, it is important to note that Herkimer used his home on the Erie Canal as a travelers' inn for refugees, those passing through the violent frontier. The site was constructed in 1764 and experienced violent raids by native tribes, countless travelers and a number of deaths as a frontier home. This can account for the numerous apparitions that are witnessed at night on the grounds, the phantom voices of women and numerous report of ghostly activity at the site.

While a site may attain recognition for the historic figures that may have visited a location it may not be that figure that is haunting the site but without those historic figures believed to haunt the locations many sites would have fewer reports and legends associated with them.

∞Folklore and Reality∞

When you get a reputation as a paranormal investigator, oftentimes people will come up to us with suggestions for places to investigate. Usually these locations will be tied to some sort of local folklore, which causes people to believe that the location is actively haunted. Sometimes we have the opportunity to look into these reports, and often what we find is not at all what the folklore says is happening. Looking at these cases, we can see that the folklore of an area is not always an accurate depiction of what is actually there.

The Remsen Stone Meeting House

The above picture was taken at the first public investigation of the Remsen Stone Meeting House, by a participant on the investigation, Lindsey Pallas. This building is an interesting case because there was no folklore involving the location.

The Remsen Stone Meeting House was an active church until the late 1980s. There were some reports of feeling watched, but nothing really concrete about the location. We decided to hold a public investigation there as a fundraiser, in the hopes that something interesting would happen, to make it worth the participant's time.

Soon after the investigation started, it became clear that the lack of folklore about the site was not an indicator that there was nothing paranormal present. Almost as soon as we started looking, people started taking interesting pictures, and reported seeing and smelling things that could not be tied to the environment.

Over the course of multiple public and private investigations, the Stone Meeting House has been proven to be an actively haunted location.

Pine Grove Cemetery

We were first introduced to Pine Grove Cemetery by our good friend and author Cheri Farnsworth, author of the *Haunted Northern New York* book series, among others. She had written about the ghosts of Pine Grove Cemetery in one of her previous books, and had suggested that we check out the cemetery and see what we could find.

According to the folklore, Pine Grove Cemetery was haunted by the spirit of a man Dragon Obretnoff, who was buried in the back of the cemetery. Dragon's headstone was noticeable not only because of his unique name, but also because the headstone was made of pink granite. Cheri had been told that people had been scared while visiting Dragon's grave by hearing a man say "Don't turn around" behind them, while they were the only ones in the cemetery.

Dragon's history was a tragic one. According to local folklore, Dragon was killed in a bar fight. The actual history shows that this was technically true, but the details of his death had become changed over time. Dragon was a man who was in the wrong place at the wrong time, and was killed as the result of the bar fight, not as the cause of the fight.

As our investigation would show, Dragon had gotten a bad reputation in the cemetery, and maybe not one that was deserved.

When we first entered the cemetery, we went immediately to Dragon's grave. Scanning with EMF, we investigated his grave and the area around it. We were surprised t o find that there were no strange EMF around his grave. As the night progressed, we soon determined why that was.

After close to three hours of investigating, we started experiencing weird activity. All of the investigators were reporting hearing strange footsteps running up to them, and abruptly stopping when the investigator would turn to look. We were also starting to hear someone whispering in our ear, trying to get our attention.

That is when we started noticing the shadow running around the cemetery. The shadow seemed to be teasing us, running all over the cemetery, moving faster the longer we tried to track it.

Interestingly enough, and what made us draw the conclusion that it was not Dragon's spirit toying with us, was that the spirit seemed to go out of its way to avoid the area of the cemetery where Dragon was buried. The spirit ran all over the cemetery, except for that location. While that does not rule out Dragon's spirit remaining at the cemetery, it seemed to indicate that Dragon's spirit is not the one toying with visitors.

Penn Mountain Cemetery

Penn Mountain Cemetery is located on a remote road outside of Remsen, New York. The folklore on the location is that the cemetery is home to a haunted rocking chair, which brings death to all who sit in it. This folklore has caused the cemetery to be a magnet for thrill-seekers who then vandalize and desecrate the grave.

The Shadow Chasers investigated this cemetery in an attempt to get to the bottom of this folklore. While we do not go to locations to purposely prove rumors wrong, we were going with the basic assumption that these reports were inaccurate, mostly due to previous acquaintance with this location.

What we found at the cemetery proved that this folklore was nothing more than rumors. There was no paranormal activity in the cemetery itself, and while we encountered what appeared to be a spirit, as shown in the picture above, but this spirit was tied more to the road that passes by the cemetery than the cemetery itself.

Hopkinton-Ft. Jackson Cemetery

This investigation is a good demonstration of just how inaccurate folklore can ultimately end up being.

The folklore associated with Hopkinton-Ft. Jackson Cemetery was that the ghost of a woman, appearing shrouded in mist, would cross the street running next to the cemetery, drift through the cemetery, and then disappear.

When we investigated, we didn't encounter any spirit activity, but when we developed the pictures after the fact, we discovered the above picture.

Looking at the picture at first, we assumed that it was the standard cemetery picture. When investigating a cemetery, you will end up with hundreds of pictures of tombstones. Looking closer, we noticed that the one on the end was see-through.

Returning to the cemetery some weeks later, we found the location of the headstones in the picture. There was no small headstone on the end. It only existed within the picture.

So, there was no misty spirit lady, but there was a very clear ghostly tombstone.

Emily's Bridge, Stowe, VT

Emily's Bridge is one of the first locations the Shadow Chasers investigated, back when our technology was limited ,and we utilized film cameras and the older style audio recorders.

The folklore of Emily's Bridge is that a girl named Emily either hung herself on the bridge, devastated over being broken up with by her boyfriend, or killed in a wagon accident, upset over being jilted by her fiancée. Emily is reported to haunt this bridge, and those who visit the bridge experience the sensation of ropes tightening around them, hear a woman's voice, or catch glimpses of a spirit.

When we investigated, we didn't find anything to indicate that there was a spirit present. After the fact, audio recordings were analyzed that appeared to have recorded the voice of a woman, but we were unable to determine anything beyond that.

Satterlee Hall – SUNY Potsdam

Phil and Kate both attended college at SUNY Potsdam, in Potsdam, NY. While they were attending college there, they did many investigations of the academic buildings on campus.

Satterlee Hall was one building that had a reputation for being haunted. The Shadow Chasers were invited to investigate the costume closet located on the second floor of the building . Workers in the costume department had reported receiving a message on their answering machine of an old woman asking for 'Audrey', and reported feeling watched while in the costume closet.

During the investigation, the team discovered that the costume closet was not haunted by the spirit of a man, as previously believed, Instead, we obtained an EVP of what sounded like a small dog barking. The costume closet was a completely internal room, with no access to the outside. There was no way that the recorder could have picked up a dog barking outside the building.

Interestingly enough, when doing follow up research on the investigation, a painting was discovered in a downstairs office in the building. The painting depicted the man whom Satterlee Hall was named after, Frank Satterlee. In the painting, he was holding a small dog, which had lived with him in the building, and had been his constant companion. Had the spirit of the dog never left the building?

Happy Valley

The Shadow Chasers were invited to come along on an investigation of Happy Valley, a forested area outside of Syracuse. When planning the investigation, we were told that Happy Valley was a village that was the site of the Black Plague, or Malaria, in the late 1800s, The entire village was killed off, and little by little nature reclaimed the land, until which time New York State purchased the land, turning it into a state park.

Since that time, it is reported that Happy Valley is aggressively haunted, and no one will stay in the park for more than a few hours.

After investigating the location, and doing further research of our own, that story has proven to be inaccurate. Not much evidence of paranormal activity was obtained outside of the cemetery located in the heart of the forest, and even the activity recorded there was nothing more than some interesting photographs and EVPs.

Doing research into the location revealed that the Great Depression had more to do with the abandonment of the site than any illness did. During the Great Depression, many farmers were unable to make a living off the land, and were forced to relocate in order to support their families. It was during this time that New York State was starting to practice reforestation, both as a way to preserve the wildlife of the state, and also to provide work.

As farmers left their Happy Valley properties, the state began to acquire those properties, returning the land to its natural state. Nothing sinister, just the progression of time.